Breaking Through Your Own Glass Ceiling

Breaking Through Your Own Glass Ceiling

Embracing a Full-hearted Life

Linda González, MSW, MFA

Library of Congress Control Number: 2020911170
ISBN: Hardcover   978-1-9845-8437-3
                   Softcover   978-1-9845-8436-6
                   eBook   978-1-9845-8435-9

Photo/Art acknowledgements:

Author photograph: Susan Raudry
Cover photograph and endless knot art illustration: Gina González-Roundey
Moon illustration: Teotli González-Roundey
What Matters photograph: Linda González

Print information available on the last page.

Rev. date: 07/21/2020

To order additional copies of this book, contact:
Xlibris
1-888-795-4274
www.Xlibris.com
Orders@Xlibris.com
814222

CONTENTS

Section 5: Consistent, Persistent Action

Dedication

For Black, Indigenous, and People of Color – thank you for staying alive and being my mirror and inspiration.

Introduction

I have been a life coach, primarily for women of color, for over twenty-five years. In that time the number one challenge my clients face is how to navigate the "glass ceilings" of society. In economics, a glass ceiling is defined as "the unseen, yet unbreachable barrier that keeps Black, Indigenous and People of Color (BIPOC) and women from rising to the upper rungs of a corporation or agency, regardless of their qualifications or achievements."

My clients never say: "I want to work on breaking through my own glass ceiling." They have other goals and are wondering why they seem to be stymied despite working hard and doing what they were told would expand opportunities for them. I understand.

My immigrant parents believed I got a better life with no glass ceiling because I was born in the U.S., learned English before I went to kindergarten, was raised in white neighborhoods, and received a formal education at Stanford and USC. Yet, like my clients, every day a moment arises when I have to justify my worth, appease people who create the glass ceilings, or be "la primera", clearing a path that was supposed to be evened out by the sacrifice of my parents, all the civil rights movements, and the letters after my name for my two masters degrees.

I have not yet, as have so many of my comadres, been mistaken for "the help", but I held many of those jobs from my early teens into my mid-twenties – maid, waitress, child care provider, home care assistant, coat check attendant, office clerk, and fast food cook. These jobs helped me finance my undergraduate and first graduate degree. I went from health care educator to social worker to my current work as a self-employed consultant, trainer, facilitator, and life coach.

Like many people wishing to understand how to navigate the unseen, yet unbreachable barriers that I face daily, I read self-help and motivational books that, while helpful, did not address my biggest challenge—working with power dynamics and a glass ceiling that fed a feeling that I might not be a smart as I thought I was. These books take a "one size fits all" approach to well-being that is inherently flawed, just like the one size fits all clothing I see occasionally. Like me, my clients engaged in the practices suggested to support their career development and self-care, but encountered subtle individual aggressions and institutions fostering a white supremacy[1] culture that values individualism, perfectionism, quantity over quality, paternalism, power hoarding, and only one right way, identified by Tema Okun of the training collaborative Dismantling Racism Works. I will be referring to this work at various points in this book so take the time to look it up. We are all susceptible to engaging in these values and behaviors, as they are baked into systems regardless of stated equity values. There is a different cost depending on your power status, including your very life. Without addressing the harm caused by those underlying values, these books sometimes increase distress for people like us, because we do what they recommend and still don't see the promised results. The erroneous conclusion is to believe we are flawed and internalize our own glass ceiling.

Because your identities determine how much privilege and discrimination you experience, the first step is to reject the idea of a 'level playing field' where all people have an equal chance at success. The data proves this. An article out of Harvard Business school states: "Companies are more than twice as likely to call minority applicants for interviews if they submit whitened resumes than candidates who

---

[1]   https://collectiveliberation.org/wp-content/uploads/2013/01/White_Supremacy_Culture_Okun.pdf

reveal their race—and this discriminatory practice is just as strong for businesses that claim to value diversity as those that don't."

It is important to replace misinformation that harms you with a vision that nurture your body, mind, and spirit. For example, a recent report on women of color in the nonprofit sector debunked widespread assumptions that there are not enough BIPOC willing and able to lead. The report called on the sector to address deeply embedded biases and systematic barriers that make it harder for BIPOC to advance into leadership positions, despite being just as qualified as their white peers.

Breaking through your own glass ceiling is critical internal work to be able to challenge these external systematic barriers. No matter how educated or professionally accomplished you may be, your race, gender, and other factors will present obstacles to your success both in and outside of the workplace. Why does this matter? These inequities lead to higher rates of depression, ill health, and lower pay rates for women and BIPOC because the status quo is not set up for our success. White women still only earn 77 cents for every dollar the average white man earns, African American women 71 cents, and Latinas 66 cents. There are multiple reasons for this, including "occupational segregation" where women are steered toward professions that pay less. Even though women earn higher grades than men, one year after graduating from college, women with a computer science degree – a high-earning field – are earning 77 cents for each $1 earned by their male classmates with the same degree. This then locks them into permanently lower pay because employers often base their salary offers on what job candidates previously earned. Third, women's earnings slip 4 percent for each child they have. Men's earnings, by comparison, get a bump when they have children. This is all exacerbated for women of color, immigrants, and for those over forty.

While it is important to fight for laws and policies that eliminate discrimination, it is equally important to do the internal work because that is where we always have agency. Because of this relentless inequity, you likely have thoughts and behaviors that discount you and those you love. (Spoiler alert: it is not because you are bad or weak.) I work with clients to leave toxic situations with power and grace and to prioritize relationships, work, and prosperity that support their long-term success.

Does this lead my clients to experience fewer obstacles? I wish I could say "Yes!". The bald truth is "No". There is still a relentless tide of either direct assaults on our communities' civil rights or backhanded compliments like: "You are so articulate." We work to acknowledge and manage obstacles sooner, rather than waiting until depleted and bitter. We analyze situations ahead of time by assessing a group or organization's demographics and values beforehand to know what level of comfort and support to expect and what strategies to have in mind.

I constantly point out to my clients that they are not the problem. In addressing the social, political and institutional forces arrayed against their well-being, I tell them, "You were not meant to survive, much less to thrive." The great Audre Lorde wrote a poem called *The Litany for Survival* that makes this perfectly clear. Accepting this reality breaks the unconscious pattern of thinking that if we try harder and sacrifice our essential self, we will be seen and valued by people with positional power. We can then proactively manage big or subtle aggressions with realistic expectations, along with strength, courage, and wisdom.

We all deserve to be respected and loved for all of who we are. OSFA self-help books and workshops inadvertently send the message that vision boards, meditation apps, and affirmations will compensate for exclusionary policies and laws. They don't prepare you for harmful behavior on the part of those with the power and privilege to, for example, be sexual predators and still hold high offices. As a woman of color and a child of immigrants, there are days when I must work extra hard to trust my truth and not give in to despair and self-blame. This is not a post-racial society. Just consider who dies disproportionately in any health crisis or police encounter.

Women and BIPOC have been colonized to think it is our limitations that cause our failures. The greatest tennis player of all time, Serena Williams, shows how insidious an internal glass ceiling can be. As she got closer to tying or breaking records by previous great players in the biggest four tournaments of each year, she shared: "I remember how stressed I was about getting to Grand Slam number eighteen," Serena said in an interview. "I had lost every Grand Slam that year. I was in the U.S. Open, and Patrick my coach, said, 'Serena, this doesn't make sense. You're so stressed about eighteen. Why not 30? Why not 40?' For me, that clicked. I won eighteen, nineteen, and 20 right after that. Why would I want to stand side by side when I can stand out on my own? I think sometimes women limit themselves."

I know we do, as do BIPOC. I use my words and wisdom so those with the biggest glass ceiling can embrace their path and shine as bright as possible. Only when people with the least privilege and access prosper can all our lives truly matter.

To change habits that do not work, you need to create structures that interrupt them and develop full-hearted alternatives.

This book offers prosperity practices my clients and I have used to successfully resist inequities when your group identities determine how much privilege and discrimination you experience. According to an analysis by Oxfam, the worth of women's yearly unpaid labor is $10.9 trillion. This exceeds the combined revenue of the 50 largest companies on 2019's Fortune Global 500 list, including Walmart, Apple, and Amazon.

There are five sections in this book, each of which focus on mindset shifts and strategies I have used and have seen bring awareness, ease, and positive results for my clients. These sections are, in and of themselves, big-picture practices to break through limiting thoughts and actions. The word *consistent* begins each section as an antidote to two white supremacy behaviors—perfectionism and a sense of urgency. There is enough time, and rather than aiming to be perfect, you aim to be consistent, which Merriam-Webster defines as "marked by harmony, regularity, or steady continuity." With a steady barrage of messages to do it right the first time, we must be compassionate when we slide down the path of perfection.

Each chapter's subject is a specific practice within the larger section practice and a response to key issues I continually work on with myself and clients. These will likely go against messages you have heard from family, friends, or authority figures. If you have, these practices will help you understand how you may have, despite your best efforts, internalized society's glass ceiling, feeding the doubt in your heart that says you are not good enough. The chapters also include an easy-to-understand *"one thing"* my clients' have said shifted their perspective, as well as stories, breakthrough prompts, and one suggested *"do it"* action. These simple, proven daily practices can release negative patterns in your life, and they require your active participation and curiosity.

You can use this book in various ways. You can start from the beginning and follow it chronologically in the flow I designed as building blocks. Or you can go to a section or chapter that calls you. Each chapter expands on the others. Each rekindles the wisdom and insights offered by the others. The book is circular, and there is no right way to use it. I would strongly recommend you read it with a journal nearby to write your responses to the "Ready for a breakthrough" questions at the end of each chapter and for anything moments when you read something that resonates with you so you can stop and dig into the soil of your heart and spirit.

The goal of this book is to make joy and rest non-negotiable in your life, no matter the waves of injustice and subtle aggressions that knock you down because you do not fit the definition of "right" in society. As the great author and social critic Claudia Rankine says in her book *Citizen*:

The worst injury is feeling you don't belong so much to you—

When you break through any aspect of your own glass ceiling, it will naturally release tiny cracks in other areas of your life and in the lives of those around you. Our efforts together multiply and expand opportunities to embrace full-hearted lives. Thank you for embarking on this journey of love, healing, and belonging with me.

Section 1

Consistent Purpose and Passion

1

Live with Purpose

> Your purpose in life is to find your purpose and give your whole heart and soul to it.
>
> —Buddha

THERE IS ABUNDANT DATA that illustrates the power of living a purposeful life. Do you know what yours is? If so, are you marshaling your energy to make it a daily reality? And if you do make your purpose a daily reality, what else have you not yet dared to do, so you can live it fully? Being grounded in your purpose means you have a compass to direct you toward a new facet of your passion, vocation, mission, and/or profession.

My own journey to a purposeful life began at a weekend workshop on breaking the chains of the internal slave mentality led by an African American man. He had graciously allowed me to attend this workshop for black people (with the permission of the other attendees) so I could see about creating a similar workshop for the Latinx community. His core exercise was for participants to write their purpose statement. These carefully chosen words, which I've periodically tweaked over the years, are the foundation of my life by design: *To work with multicultural wisdom and balance and inspire Black,*

Indigenous and People of Color (BIPOC) to embark on a creative, cooperative journey of love and healing for this and future generations.

These words serve as an inner touchstone to guide my actions. My purpose statement is in the bio I send to clients, right alongside the technical and sector skills I bring. I feel vulnerable acknowledging that if I work with you or your organization, my purpose is an essential part of my skill set, along with my creative mind and spirited energy. It does not fit into the standard notion of a bio, but I have decided again and again that it is a risk I embrace.

Living a purposeful life means continually committing to the circumstances that will allow your best self to thrive despite barriers based on race, gender identity, and other oppressions. If you were trained to obey authority or only feel validated by external recognition, creating a purposeful life will mean shifting slowly to being guided by your internal compass. You take on your life as your responsibility. Your purpose establishes the direction you will take regardless of changing causes and conditions, income streams and supervisors, or cities and relationships.

You can choose to have your life be an expression of what you love doing and what benefits you and others. By default, you may have elected to have someone else make the selection for you. That too is a decision, albeit often an unconscious one. Why would you choose to abandon your purpose for another person's? First, you may have had limiting beliefs planted in your mind, usually very early in life, that you were not allowed to have your own path. As children, many of us got that message, which was reinforced in schools and workplace hierarchies. If you consider immigration status, gender, and class, just to name a few factors that send these types of messages, then your life can rightfully feel like a commodity for someone else's benefit. Having a clear sense of your purpose disrupts that narrow mentality and opens new possibilities.

I fought for my right to express my opinions and values as a child and was consistently punished by authority figures for doing so. Even when I added the external validation of a master's degree in social work, I was suspended, demoted, and fired as an adult for challenging my supervisors about program or staffing inequities in order to improve morale and provide culturally competent services. Wounded but undaunted, I chose self-employment so that I could determine my work life trajectory with added agency. I slowly built a solid business working in the field of equity by providing trainings, consultation, and coaching in numerous sectors. The original joy and passion for this work slipped through my fingers with each client contact. While the organizations I worked with made changes, their leaders were white and would decide at some point they had done enough. Rather than acknowledging their discomfort with dismantling structural inequities that served them and people like them, they would end our contracts even though we had fulfilled our agreed upon outcomes.

My purpose practice drove me to make a change. Several, in fact. I came to understand that my particular purpose was best served as a solo practitioner with a focus on coaching, writing, and working with organizations led by BIPOC. I flew cross-country every six months for two years to complete my MFA in Creative Writing, returning to my early passion to be an author. I wanted my twins to see a vibrant parent who believed in her right to love and joy despite the daily obstacles I faced as a greying woman of color.

Many of my clients work with me to develop their authentic diverse voice and leadership in a minefield of inequities. One had begun a job tasked with shifting the organization's main strategy and integrating work across programs. Her leadership style was different than the charismatic white male CEO beloved by the board of directors.

THAT ONE THING... Linda's thoughtful coaching had me align my purpose with my position and develop my unique leadership style. As the organization shifted its mission and services, it guided me to make compromises in the institutional structure only so far as I knew I was where I needed to be, and my leadership was seen and supported.

By looking at the world through a purposeful lens, you simplify and improve the quality of your life and increase time in expanded energy fields like peace, joy, and love. This does not mean you discount the importance of feeling your fear, anger, and grief. Current and historical inequities are baked into institutional policies. Even if affirmative action was understood or utilized well, leaders still preference their own comfort and want people who will fit into their culture. So many of my clients, as well as I, have been hired to add a missing diversity demographic. When we speak authoritatively, grounded in our lived experience and educational knowledge, we are told to "tone it down."

> With a purpose inspiring abundance, courage, and discipline, you can then refuse to cater to this culture of scarcity and competition.

With a purpose inspiring abundance, courage, and discipline, you can then refuse to cater to this culture of scarcity and competition. It may mean seeking another work environment, but not because you failed to find the perfect words to convince your bosses your view was valid. You see clearly you were wanted for a finite reason, not for your full self. Many of my clients are social justice change agents and have a difficult time tuning into their purpose beyond direct action and services for people failed by the educational, immigration, and justice systems. They worry about being selfish if they consider what they want for themselves. I encourage them to explore what they love first, reminding them they will always integrate justice and equity into their decisions, no matter where they work and live. I remind parents that keeping their children safe and educating them on racial justice issues is often an invisible and essential part of their purpose.

I have my coaching clients complete a purpose statement worksheet; many resist because it makes them put down in writing what matters most to them. They then must use it to make decisions rather than hope something they care about will come along. One client told me a few years after I had him do the worksheet how much he didn't want to name his purpose because it took concentrated effort to get the words to match his core values. He said he really appreciated it now to guide his current work and to help him consider future possibilities.

Clients usually know what they don't want. Confirming our "no" is frequently the door to confirming our "yes." Curiosity and investigation are necessary prerequisites to forge a purpose statement that is specific enough to guide you and broad enough to offer many opportunities. It includes your unique qualities and gifts, whose lives you want to impact, and what will be different as a result of your efforts. We accept the importance of loving, committed relationships to others, yet give up the possibility of a loving, committed relationship to our purpose and our gifts. Someone who does this is Robin Wall Kimmerer, the author of *Braiding Sweetgrass: Indigenous Wisdom, Scientific Knowledge and the Teachings of Plants* and an enrolled member of the Citizen Potawatomi Nation; she combines her heritage with her scientific and environmental passions. Her quote sums up the function of your purpose: "All the elements are in place. But without the spark it is only a pile of dead sticks. So much depends on the spark."

Once decided, living out your purpose is the spark that turns dead sticks into fire.

When we are hindered by the limitations of a situation, our diminished inner fire should alert us to return to our purpose. It means lowering the volume on the commercials that try to convince us that a raise or a certificate of recognition or a few more vacation days will ease the discomfort in our souls. These "golden handcuffs" tempt us to stay bound to external rewards that limit us and keep us from nurturing ourselves. (I address this throughout the book.)

My nephew, who does strength training regularly, told me that we all have a six-pack—those muscles are there. Your purpose is like your abdominal muscles. The issue is whether you or anyone else can see them, and most important, whether you are using them to keep you balanced and strong. When your purpose is exercised, your "why" is consistently evident to others.

However, the stronger you get, the more your life will ask of you. I learned this in strength training, Buddhist meditation, and in my yoga practice. I was sure it would all get easier with practice and devotion. It only became easier when I stopped thinking about a linear "end" and focused on self-awareness with a beginner's mind. I am always arriving at a new learning edge and understanding of what it takes to deepen my practice.

If you have a hard time starting to develop your purpose statement, ask yourself: When did I know I was in my truth? What moments in my life engaged me fully – body, mind, and spirit?

I will share one here. During winter break of my last year at Stanford University, I decided to volunteer on Skid Row in a soup kitchen. I went one morning to help prepare and serve a meal to homeless people. I smelled of onions and the grit of downtown Los Angeles, but I was exhausted and in bliss driving home to West Los Angeles.

I meant to go only one day but ended up going back every day for a week, rising early when I could have slept in, and working hard when I could have been watching TV. The key gears of what would become my purpose were being greased.

Purpose both directs your course like a sail and is your anchor in difficult times when you need to seek protection and hold space for your experiences. The bigger your ship of life and the longer the journey, the bigger your anchor must be. We typically grow our ship of life without growing our anchor at the same pace. Some of you are prone to sail past harbors, barreling ahead toward their intended destination until they sink into physical, mental or emotional illness. Some of you never leave the harbor for fear you are not ready. Which is your tendency?

The length and difficulty of our journey determines how long we need to be in harbor: restocking supplies, healing heart wounds, and gathering the right team for our next journey.

When living your purpose, there are truths that stay firm in any situation and some factors that are fluid depending on the circumstances. As you continue to grow into your purpose, you will come to know what is non-negotiable and where you can be flexible.

Ready for a #fullhearted breakthrough?

The words that come up when I think of my purpose are...

The first step I can take to grow my anchor is...

The people who help me heal and replenish when I need a harbor are...

Do it.

Craft a one sentence purpose that names your special contributions and for whom you focus your efforts and get support and feedback from several trusted colleagues/friends.

2

Embrace Your "Body of Life"

Don't ask what the world needs. Ask what makes you come alive, and go do it. Because what the world needs is people who have come alive.

— Howard Thurman

WHAT DOES IT MEAN to have a "body of life"—the space and time to encompass your purpose and passions? What happens when you stop thinking that one person, job, home, car, educational achievement, or external recognition will confirm your essential goodness?

We may have heard of a "body of work", defined loosely as the entirety of the creative or academic output produced by an individual or unit. This is usually used for professionals in a specific field, but can include different arenas given the changes in the work environment where people blend different ways of working. My "body of work" will be, in its most concrete form, books and the channels I use to leverage my stories and the lessons I continue to learn, as well as the speeches, courses, and personal conversations that inspire people to take *their* "body of life" seriously.

A "body of life" encompasses achievements that are connected to your purpose. It is not a resume, although some elements may show up there. It is what you do with all your heart, mind, and spirit. It is what stretches you further than you ever imagined and allows you to give and receive with respect and joy. A "body of life" is focused on creating a legacy, defined as something handed down from an ancestor or preceding generations, an inheritance, a birthright. This is often narrowly seen as being connected to wealth or property, and my frame is to include anything that endures beyond your lifetime.

My "body of life" has multiple components—all are directly tied to my purpose. Two examples are my children and my creative work. My twins are in their twenties and embarking on their journeys beyond my constant caregiving and direction. Having dedicated myself to them beyond what I could have imagined, I am excited to see what unfolds with their decision-making and the set of values they have inherited from their parents, their culture, and their larger family and community.

Having a "body of life" requires great discipline and unerring belief in your dreams. After he won his first Oscar as a director, Ang Lee said: "I struggled through six years of agonizing, hopeless uncertainty." I could say that about my first book, substituting thirteen for six! Are you willing to endure

> Having a "body of life" requires great discipline and unerring belief in your dreams.

that kind of explicit uncertainty to achieve one of your goals? If you can admit that uncertainty is inherent in life, you are more likely to reach a place of fruition because you know change is inherent in any choice. It will mean you have done whatever it takes to truly enjoy the culmination of your efforts—and then you can get back to work on another aspect of your "body of life."

Both Ang Lee and I, as BIPOC, had to sail beyond what our parents, family, and friends deemed reasonable. I had no "steady job," no determined career ladder, no day like any other (friends thought I was involved in pyramid schemes). To live my full-hearted "body of life," I had to release the power of others' opinions and trust my inner compass.

Being a lifelong learner is essential to creating a "body of life"; it means you are not thwarted by failure and the sight of yet another starting line. When you stop buying the "pleasing others" brand of fuel to drive your life, you will be able to listen to your internal warning signs to avoid detours and stay on your chosen path.

People may not like the mirror you hold up because of how your choices reflect on their own. Much of this will feel like rain on your parade. Notice the normal pull to get sidetracked because it feels easier than discovering and living your "body of life." Refusing to conform to the norm is a marathon and takes planning and commitment over the long term, with scheduled stops for replenishment.

I worked with a client who was hired at a high level in a museum to direct their education program because of her equity lens. When she named the "public" they were doing community outreach to as BIPOC, she was told by her CEO that she was calling out the other leadership staff as racist. The CEO then told her not to come to a board meeting because what they said might "offend" her—continually calling her "unprofessional" when she raised the issues she was hired to address and making her the problem. We were focused on documenting her accomplishments, connecting with other women of color who had been pushed out, and looking for other work that supported her "body of life" when the CEO "restructured" my client's job and laid her off.

THAT ONE THING… As I worked through a situation where I was not given the resources to succeed, Linda told me not to expect equity when it was not possible. She encouraged me to focus instead on prioritizing my non-negotiables and reminded me "professional" is often code for white supremacy.

Focus on what is enduring and nurtures your soul. It is our birthright to be brilliant, healthy, and full of joy. And remember, life is inherently unstable; it is our purpose and "body of life" that make our path stable. Most people can get laid off tomorrow, and we who work for ourselves could find ourselves with no clients or students. Embracing your "body of life" does not make the grind of daily tasks, the grief of loss, or the outrage of injustice disappear. It does allow you to feel all of it—the delight and disappointment—and still stay on your path because you know how to pivot when necessary.

Believe that your truth matters. As Eleanor Roosevelt said: "The future belongs to those who believe in the beauty of their dreams."

Ready for a #fullhearted breakthrough?
I can be distracted from my dreams by...
My non-negotiables to achieve my dreams are...
To achieve one aspect of my "body of life," I must learn about...

Do it.
Make a list of two to three core elements of your "body of life".

3

Know Your True Prosperity

If you don't get out there and define yourself, you'll be quickly and inaccurately defined by others.

—Michelle Obama

AMID A CHALLENGING WORK situation, a trusted colleague asked me: "Where do you shine?" That short question meant many things: What are the circumstances that allow your body, mind, and spirit to prosper? Where are you emotionally and physically safe and secure? Where can you learn and grow in an honest and supportive manner?

The daily pull of external and internal expectations can cloud your vision until you are depleted and unconsciously reverting to survival habits. This can show up as saying "yes" without thoroughly examining the pros and cons of a situation, group, or relationship. You may, as I have surely done, excuse inadequate communication, tolerate missed commitments, and spend precious time processing the past to avoid making decisions about a toxic situation. You can only do this if you know where you shine and believe in your right to prosper.

To understand how to bloom in different environments, first define what constitutes sunlight, nutrients, and water for you—the necessary elements for you to prosper. It is your responsibility to pursue what you need, and that will mean uprooting yourself when what you thought was an oasis turns out to be hard clay. You will respond quickly to nourishment if you recommit to your right to prosper rather than sink into self-blame.

> To understand how to bloom in different environments, first define what constitutes sunlight, nutrients, and water for you—the necessary elements for you to prosper.

Think about where you may have let yourself and your gifts be diminished and decide what seeds of action you can plant today to prepare for a future harvest. A Chinese proverb sums it up beautifully: "All the flowers of all the tomorrows are in the seeds of today." This is an antidote to the "get rich quick" paradigms that ignore glass ceilings.

One of the internal obstacles that can be a barrier to prosperity is not understanding how a tool can become your master. For example, the Internet, social media, and your mobile phone are tools to support your prosperity, not dictate your life and energy decisions. Yet they are tempting as distractions when waves of despair knock you down. Many people tell me how much they hate social media because it is a time suck. I encourage them to shift so rather than it being a master of their time, it is a tool for their goals. People think because I am active on social media that I must be spending hours on it. I tell them I usually spend a focused, strategic fifteen minutes a day. I know my purpose and I design my time in advance rather than use it to distract me. A different and prevalent tool is pride, as it can support or derail your prosperity depending on whether driven by your ego or appropriate appreciation of your efforts. I learned this the hard way many years ago.

I auditioned to be a host for a career-path series that would be aired on a public television station. I had been a career counselor/ coach for many years and enjoy being on stage. The producers were pleased with my presentation and told me they would be offering me the job. A few days later they called to say they had to withdraw their offer because I did not have a degree specific to the field. I became outraged, feeling that my experience and my master's degree in a related field should be enough. They wanted to figure out a way for me to be able to do at least some of the work, but my pride, driven by ego, turned from being a tool to being my master. I refused to agree to any changes, sticking to my stance that my credentials were enough for them to take me as I was. They decided to keep looking and I was left having dinner alone with my bruised ego.

Embracing an abundant definition of prosperity means seeing life as full of options rather than a right/wrong paradigm. Even when you are reaching your goals, you remain open to reassessing and asking yourself: Is this work or community activity still nurturing my purpose? Further, you are open to releasing your current success for something that will allow you to make a prosperity leap. That means being willing to do the grunt work that nobody sees in order to shift your course. It also requires taking risks and learning from each failure. If you don't have generational wealth in your family or community to fund you or fall back on, glass ceilings make risks higher—privilege is an invisible safety net. Therefore, much of my work with clients is supporting them to slowly make shifts so they can move into arenas where they can prosper in the future while they remain in their current situation. Prosperity is a long, unsteady process that will have its ups and downs. That is where leaning on your purpose and community for guidance is essential.

To fully espouse prosperity, start by taking a thoughtful, honest look at your financial health. What is your basic spending plan, the one that covers your essentials each month? Have you explored what businessman and author Robert Kiyosaki, of *Rich Dad Poor Dad* fame, calls the cash flow quadrant and determined a plan for generating income apart from trading your time for money? What is the glass ceiling you have placed above yourself, the maximum amount of money you would allow yourself to generate?

Women talk about the glass ceiling and bemoan sexism all the time. I did too, but it took me a long time to finally look up at my internalized glass ceiling. My limiting belief about what I could earn was about $80,000 a year, just a little higher than what I had ever earned. Why? Because it would create ease without allowing me to dream or act big. I felt out the contours of my glass ceiling without self-blame, remembering the societal injustices I had experienced that forged it. I was then free to harness my energy to instead break through this ceiling.

Your aspiration is to keep growing into the fullness of your gifts with no timeframe for success. This debunks the scarcity and urgency paradigms that push us to make decisions based in fear. Be aware that if your prosperity mindset gets bigger, people who are still caught in their self-limiting beliefs will get scared. You may be met with verbal or nonverbal messages like: *Why do you care so much? Why can't you stay in one job? That seems unrealistic. Can you tone it down?*

These are external messages they internalized in order to survive. Self-talk gone wrong. No one is born with these thoughts; they come from a dominant culture that has standards about who can be big and who needs to settle for less. I pointed out to a client that people both love her courage and are also scared when she brings up something that shows she is "outside the box" and "ahead" of them. By not settling for lower expectations of herself, she did not receive full support from either her leadership team or her colleagues to grow her gifts.

When you act in pursuit of your true prosperity, people will see you shine and want to engage with you. For myself, I am careful about joining new groups because it is likely I will be tapped to be in a leadership position. Taking on such a role is a thoughtful decision based on other goals and aspirations I have for my work, creative life, community, and family. This means managing my generous tendency to give to a cause or group that is special to me. Sometimes it all works out well and sometimes it doesn't. That does not mean I'm not on my prosperity path, it just means I must slow down, check in with my purpose, and reset my expectations.

One of the best ways to sustain and protect a prosperity mindset is to make preparation a consistent habit before moving to action. Some for me are to make a call before going to a store to confirm they have what I want or make sure the restaurant is open, check the weather to figure out the best way to dress, have the right equipment for my activity, ponder what could go wrong, and pack water and snacks!

You will sometimes feel the thud of a real glass ceiling when you go against the dominant culture's notion of how much you can prosper, based on dynamics of power and privilege. This will be a reminder of the delusion of a linear, upward one size fits all path. Expect this and be ready to hold fiercely to your purpose and "body of life" instead of fulfilling other people's dreams.

A client was struggling to align her own definition of prosperity against low expectations of her success and value as a black woman. I encouraged her to acknowledge but not be foiled by the different circumstances the world had of her.

> *THAT ONE THING... Linda assisted me to understand how to "set my table" – daily rituals to stay centered and focused on goals that motivated me to grow a new branch on my tree of life despite an environment polluted with anti-Blackness and oppression.*

Refuse to reside in pseudo-communities that have a narrow definition of prosperity; instead seek out those who believe in and are acting on living a self-defined, community-rich life. I used to be annoyed at weeds clawing their way through the pavement or sidewalks. Now I cheer them on as sure signs that the tiny seeds that slid into the cracks are like our determination to define our true prosperity despite small and large obstacles.

Ready for a #fullhearted breakthrough?

I let others define my right to prosperity when...

People who inspire me with their prosperity mindset are...

My gifts are received with open arms by...

Do it.

Research the Cash Flow Quadrant until you can explain it, or if you know it, share it with someone.

4

Use Money as Energy

In all realms of life it takes courage to stretch your
limits, express your power, and fulfill your potential…
it's no different in the financial realm.

—Suze Orman

YOU MAY HAVE HEARD the phrase "money is the root of all
evil." The original quote is from the book of Timothy in the
Bible: "For the *love* of money is the root of all evil." You may, like
so many people from communities without historical privilege, have
an uncomfortable relationship with money and therefore wealth.
But what underlies that uncomfortable relationship? And what is an
alternative approach that could nourish your life and break through
old thinking that limits your prosperity? Why can't you use money
as energy to fulfill your purpose?

Another way of saying this is: Your wealth is measured by how
much you have that cannot be taken away, which can include your
financial, spiritual, and emotional assets. How you feel about what
you have is within your power, even if current inequities limit your
earning capacity and harm your emotional well-being. You cannot
make changes until you commit to what creates abundance in all

areas of your life—but first, you need to explore and shift why you're not already using money as energy.

One client stated her discomfort starkly: "Having money means giving up your life." Really? Probing further, I saw some form of this thinking pattern among other clients and people in my life. Their root belief was that money was inherently tied to greed and resulted in wealth for the 1 percent and poverty for others. This dichotomy creates a false choice—be rich and greedy or be poor and noble. This played out both with people who worked directly in social justice arenas and with those who were focused on accumulating a steady paycheck; they began to earn a good income and then unconsciously found ways to not accumulate wealth because that would be giving up their "struggle." There are always family members, friends, or GoFundMe campaigns that need our help. There are cars, clothes, and trips we want to take. Not accumulating an emergency fund and other financial measures can work until a crisis hits—be it medical, familial, economic, and/or political—leaving us back at square one.

This same client recounted a time when she was in Los Angeles working as a teacher near where buildings were burning during the Rodney King riots. She and her husband left the area to visit her aunt in a suburb. When they arrived, she saw her aunt in an idyllic setting, outside watering her nice green lawn. This juxtaposition solidified her belief that money stops you from understanding suffering and working to create access for all. She presumed she had to be fighting all the time or she would lose her soul to money and greed.

The problem is an either/or framework about people based on their income. People who may be poor financially can have a joy and contentment that is far more genuine than people who are wealthy. People who have incredible financial wealth may never feel it is enough, enjoy the ease it can bring or see how it can benefit others. But that doesn't mean not having money is good, or that having money is bad. The first step to eliminating discomfort with money is seeing it as neutral. It is merely a vehicle through which energy is exchanged.

One of the reasons you may struggle with money is that your baseline needs have been consistently at risk in your life. I have had clients who supported their families in and outside the U.S., as well as some managing relatives' mental health issues and criminal arrests. Risking money in hand for the possibility of a larger return through business or investment income streams seems foolish with this reality. You are not just chancing your own finances; you see the potential impact on current familial and community stress. And if your life is focused on benefiting others, this is a huge stretch.

Your relationship with money is problematic when used as *the* vehicle for getting your higher needs met, such as love, belonging, and esteem. Make no mistake, financial well-being can support these higher-level needs, but it neither guarantees nor keeps you from meeting them. In a dominant culture laced with greed, embracing money as energy is difficult. I always ask my clients, 90 percent of whom are women and BIPOC, to tell me how they manage their money and how similar it is to their parents. The most consistent answer from my clients is that their parents lived frugally and had very little. They themselves often only make sure what they are earning covers their expenses, and in this, I cannot judge. I lived for years with no plan or goals to further my prosperity, financial and otherwise.

I changed slowly. First, I created a savings account with a three months' emergency fund. I bought term life insurance when my twins were born, eliminating it when my and their other parent's assets were enough to cover their needs. I hired a financial planner when I received an inheritance. I educated myself on the use of my money, which went against many paradigms I'd inherited from my family and community, including a steady, long-term job, retirement savings, and a focus on buying a house and spending thirty years paying for it.

The biggest one concerned my mortgage. I almost sputtered when my financial planner told me to pay it off. "What about the tax benefits?" My planner calmly said: "Take the money you would be using for mortgage payments and invest it so you earn what the tax benefits would have been. You'll have plenty, because of all the interest you won't pay over a thirty-year mortgage."

Then I read a book by Suze Orman that affirmed that the value of financial planning was first and foremost to take care of those we loved.

I could get behind that! I hired an estate attorney to create a trust so my family and twins would have a roadmap for what to do with my assets when I died. My siblings and I later used this planner to work through my parents' trust, and then both my sister and brother used her services. Going through the discomfort of facing my relationship with money and knowing how to share that with others, including family, friends, and coaching clients has created ripple effect that is exciting to watch.

One final change for me was establishing an ethical relationship with how I spend money. Knowing that there is nowhere near a level playing field in society has led me to practice affirmative action in my spending. I make sure the people who provide me with services reflect those who experience the biggest pay gap differences in society. External barriers—including social norms, biases, and the "good old boys' network," —makes it easier to buy into the belief that money is the root of all evil. It is not money that is evil, it is an adherence to the false notion that prosperity is only about material accumulation and greed.

My client's beliefs (and my previous ones) feed into a culture of scarcity and struggle. When you have these feelings and receive money, the tendency is to move it along, thereby ensuring that you will not have wealth, maintaining your personal glass ceiling. As people of heart, justice, and compassion, my clients can feel embarrassed to have abundance when others have so much less.

Have you asked yourself what is the limit of what you can earn and not feel like a sellout? Talking about money and salaries is usually considered off-limits because of this invisible ceiling and the fear one's politics will be questioned. If you are an artist, the message is even stronger that you cannot earn a lot of money.

When I decided to move to Marin County, one of the wealthiest counties in the country, some of my friends were horrified. Why? Because they labeled it as off-limits for being too white, rich, and beautiful. I was undeterred, as I had decided that I wanted to live where I went for replenishment amid the beauty of the Pt. Reyes seashore and the majestic sunsets over Mt. Tamalpais. I told people if more BIPOC moved to Marin it would become more diverse, even as I understood why they didn't.

By staying at a low income due to internally imposed limitations, your focus is necessarily on self-worth, survival, the right to take up space, and the right to be safe. Therefore, it is never the right time to embrace the abundance of the whole world without thinking you will die or be a sellout. This cannot change without a powerful shift in your relationship with money. This means fulfilling what is in your power within an inequitable system. To do this, you must release internalized group-identity stereotypes. Reflect on what you were taught and decide what is helpful and what is based in fear and past realities that have changed.

I had a client who said she wanted to leave a job but kept failing to fulfill her commitments. I dug deeper about what was blocking her from breaking through her limiting beliefs and changing what was in her power to change. This meant opening herself to seeing other riches in her life to help fuel her financial prosperity.

THAT ONE THING... Linda had me name the goodies of holding on to a job I said I wanted to leave. The list included feeling noble, thinking that wearing myself out was meaningful, that this was punishment, and if I was really doing good work, I wouldn't make good money. She helped me see that I was rich in social and human capital. I could then slowly create and act on new thoughts of prosperity.

Money is fluid, and to generate more than the basics in your life will require a different kind of risk than continuing to live under your glass ceiling. Actively educate yourself on your preferred means of generating significant residual income. Individual Retirement Accounts [IRAs], money market accounts, and Certificates of Deposits [CDs] do not count as their limited capacity to grow your money means they lack the power to significantly affect your current quality of life. Commit to educating

> *Money is fluid, and to generate more than the basics in your life will require a different kind of risk than continuing to live under your glass ceiling.*

yourself until you understand that money is not a stable entity that we can possess and fully control. I still struggle to take risks because I understand that financial abundance has a learning curve for someone like me who has had to learn all this as an adult. However, I move forward because continuing to "playing it safe" has a cost as well and is based on scarcity. The value of savings accounts, houses, and other traditional channels of generating wealth will always go up and down—they are not guaranteed. While I have lost money as I searched for ways to diversify my income streams and create passive income, I have gained a greater understanding of how money works and how to use it to further justice is what drives me. There are no guarantees you will pick right the first or second or even third investment opportunity. That is true in all aspects of our lives, including love relationships, work, and housing. Educating yourself means understanding just how unlevel the playing field is and the invisible parts of white intergenerational wealth. Though it is scary to strategically "gamble with your money" if you come from a background of scarcity, it's essential to self-determine a larger vision of prosperity.

What is guaranteed is that you will learn important lessons to share with others and you will not let someone else dictate what you do with your money. Using money as energy is well worth the effort—and it must begin by breaking through scarcity thoughts to make way for a broader horizon of possibilities. When you embrace money as energy, you can make what you do with money a reflection of your values.

Ready for a #fullhearted breakthrough?

My biggest fear about financial wealth is…

I can use my money to create…

The first step I can take to learn about money management is…

Do it.

Create a spending plan or share the one you have with someone else so they can learn.

Section 2

Consistent Nourishment

5

Find Your Breath

Feelings come and go like clouds in a windy sky.
Conscious breathing is my anchor.

— Thich Nhat Hanh

WHAT IS BREATH TO you? You can ponder this every second of every day. Like most people, I was not raised to breathe deeply and understand how this positively influences our brains and overall health. It has only been through a dedicated yoga and meditation practice that I have come to experience the power of breath and understand how crucial it is in nourishing my body, mind, and spirit.

One Saturday, I woke up with a well-defined plan. I drove to my yoga studio. After parking my car, I realized I had forgotten my yoga mat and felt irritated that I would have to pay for a loaner mat because I had not been mindful enough to bring it. As I locked the car door, a woman said: "Do you know you have a flat tire?"

"I didn't. Thank you!"

With a big sigh, I unlocked the door and sat back down. I now knew the warning light I had not understood meant I had a tire inflation issue. I sank into the disappointment of missing my class and having to go to the rental agency to get another car. But then I remembered an email I had received the day before from a friend asking for prayers for a mother whose daughter had been missing for five days. I took a breath, set aside this inconvenience, and called my VISA company to use their emergency road service. When they said there was a $60 charge to change the tire, I debated changing the tire myself, but decided against it. Meanwhile, I heard the edge of irritation in my voice as I answered the woman's questions. (Do you ever do that to customer service people? You know it is not their fault, but they are the ones saying what you don't want to hear.) I pulled away from that edge in my voice until my tone was calm, reminding myself I was safe and didn't have a daughter who was missing.

The tow-truck man came and looked at the tire.

"That is a big nail!" he said, pointing to the large head in the tire. He jacked up the car and used his high-powered tool to unscrew the lug nuts. "These are on really tight." I was glad I had called him, imagining myself trying to take them off with a small hand tool I kept in my car and the curses that would have spewed out of my mouth.

As I drove out of the parking lot, I felt tears falling from my eyes and my heart cracking open when I thought I should feel calm. Instead of figuring out the root of the tears, I started saying: "I am suffering, I am suffering, I am suffering." Suddenly a laugh interrupted me. That laugh was like someone reaching down and pulling me out of the water. That laugh made me breathe. It was the laugh of perspective amid my mind's self-created drama, knowing I had a choice to not accept a negative storyline and instead reflect on what helps me find my breath. As I drove across the Richmond bridge in the slow lane with my donut tire, I looked out at the bay and asked myself: "What helps me when I am in a place where I cannot hold on to beauty and faith and gratitude?"

First and foremost, breathing deeply. I hold my breath when my heart feels attacked as a conditioned defense mechanism, and that cuts off oxygen to my brain. Perspective is another hand that pulls me up—like thinking about that mother who did not know where her daughter was for five days. Perspective reminds me I am not the only person feeling minor annoyance or even despair. I was able to ponder the ways I find my breath as I transitioned onto the 80 freeway. As I do most mornings, I had gotten up that morning, expressed gratitude for being alive, and set my timer to meditate for twenty minutes, counting my in-breath and out-breath to ten. When I noticed I was on number seventeen or thirty-four, I returned to one.

Another way I find my breath is thinking of my millennial twins, embarking on their own journeys to find the hands in life that will pull them up to breathe when they go underwater. Sometimes the world gives us incredible hurdles and we do feel like we are drowning, like we cannot breathe. Finding your breath is an essential skill in these moments.

Understanding your relationship to breath and breathing means understanding how you may have internalized limitations from a society that rarely gives you the emotional and psychological space to breathe fully and relax your tension enough to access your heart and mind wisdom. Finding your breath means looking at the larger picture and being one with every single detail. My Buddhist practice has taught me that being present in each action allows me to stay present when life swings me by the tail. To make a good cup of tea, I have to be that tea and the cup. I have to be the hot water. Sometimes I am the honey and spoon and coconut creme. I have to know I am part of everything to access my breath in times of struggle. Looking up at the vastness of the sky or tall trees helps me remember to breathe.

To change your breath habits, notice what happens when you don't breathe properly. Shallow breathing is an uncomfortable habit that deprives you of the oxygen required by your mind and body. It is like driving with the parking brake on: You are moving, but you are causing damage to yourself that will ultimately cause harm to your body, mind, and spirit. Without enough oxygen, your brain makes mistakes that lead to poorly thought-out comments or dangerous behaviors. It leads to overreacting or underreacting, to fighting, fleeing, or freezing.

A client was struggling to adjust to the COVID-19 Shelter in Place reality, thinking she could wait it out instead of embracing the changes and making decisions based on what was real now. She was holding her breath and keeping her life in pause.

> *THAT ONE THING… Linda helped me see I could still live my life and make decisions even with no clear view of the future. She reminded me it was like driving in the fog. I could still get where I wanted; I just had to slow down, maybe choose a different route, or even pull over and rest. Safety was the highest good while I still pursued my goals.*

Claiming your breath infuses you with a physical sensation and mental belief that you can regain your balance.

Claiming your breath infuses you with a physical sensation and mental belief that you can regain your balance. The phrase: "I couldn't help myself" is never true—even in situations where you feel powerless. My clients often raise challenging situations when they felt like they had their breath taken away, especially with power dynamics.

They will ask me whether I think race was part of the equation. I say that race is always in play. The question is: How *much* of the situation was tainted by racism? Even though we know race is a social construct, it plays a role in every encounter. It could be 5 percent or 50 percent or 100 percent. There is no "race card," there is only the tragic reality that race is still one of the major rules of the game that determines your access to resources and justice.

In a society where incidents like the death of George Floyd often trigger vicarious trauma for BIPOC, you must believe in your right to stay alive. These constant personal and community assaults will crack open your heart with despair, but it will never break because you no longer accede to the paradigm that you are broken. I quote the amazing writer, producer, director, and distributor of independent film, Ava DuVernay, all the time: "It's not a broken system. It was built this way. It was built to function exactly as it is." The system we live in was set up to both exclude and privilege specific groups of people.

By the end of that Saturday I had heard the daughter was returned safely to her mother and I was in a rental car with four good tires. Doing the task before me is a door back into my breath practice. The bigger the challenges around us, the more we need to break down our days into manageable bits. Breath is always accessible, and conscious breathing is one of our most powerful antidotes to the traumas that are a daily part of life.

Ready for a #fullhearted breakthrough?

I lose my breath when...

Practices that help me incorporate deeper breathing are...

When I breathe deeply I can...

Do it.

Commit to a specific breath practice every day and set your alarms to remind you.

6

Grow to Your Full Size

How can you know what you're capable of if you
don't embrace the unknown?

—Esmeralda Santiago

THERE IS A STORY I sometimes tell my clients to explain
what it means to grow to your full size. Once upon a time there
was a tuna who lived in the Gulf of México, whom I will call Tunita.
She cavorted with her friends and grew from her juvenile size of half
an inch to two feet long at a year and half old. She and her group
were shoaling, swimming independently, but in such a way that
they stayed connected, forming a social group that provided defense
against predators and enhanced their foraging for smaller fish, squid,
crustaceans, and plankton. Tunita did not know how big a tuna
grew to be in the wild, because 90 percent of the worldwide catch of
Pacific bluefin tuna are less than two years old and under three feet
long. She did not know that she could live over twenty years, weigh
a thousand pounds, and be nine to thirteen feet in length.

Tunita swam across the gulf with her shoal to cross the Atlantic
Ocean and feed off the coast of Europe; then swam back to the gulf
to breed. Why go so far and risk so much? Because that area was their

best feeding grounds. Tunita didn't know it, but she was the Ferrari of the ocean—sleek, powerful, and made for speed up to forty-three miles an hour. Her torpedo-shaped body, still growing, streamlined through the water, and her special swimming muscles enabled her to cruise the ocean highways with great efficiency. She swam with bigger tunas who had made the passage before.

Sadly for Tunita and her friends, tuna highways had become a series of giant nets and endless lines of fishing boats. People resorted to high-tech methods to catch Tunita, including devices that herded the fish so that more could be caught. One day, after the tuna shoal rounded Florida, Tunita was caught in a net that tugged her up into the air with her friends and the bigger tunas. Just as they were about to be dropped onto the deck of a boat, she wriggled free and dropped back into the ocean. Her size saved her that time, but she remained in constant danger of not growing to her full size. She and her shoal's yearly journey to their best feeding grounds continued, and she grew to be ten feet in length.

We too can meet the fate of Tunita's friends and die having only grown to one third of our potential size. When I was young, I had amazing dreams. Then, like most of us, I was caught in a net of imposed obligations, other people's dreams, or the limitations placed on me by the persistence of gender, race, and class inequities. I didn't notice my growth had slowed down or stopped because people like me were about the same size and I thought it was normal to lower my aspirations and play small. I stopped making the effort to reach my best feeding grounds because of the times I was punished for daring to point out inequities or push for my leadership to be acknowledged. When someone "larger than life" with my characteristics appeared, I saw them as an outlier or an exception. I did not see them as a role model or proof I could reach my best feeding grounds.

Unlike Tunita and the tunas who face extinction, my nets were in my mind and heart. As I learned about glass ceilings, I understood and practiced better strategies to escape my internal nets and those that tried to trap me. Then and now, I constantly seek the best environments to thrive because the risk is worth the benefits. It has meant leaving my shoals to find other big tunas when my own stopped growing or felt threatened by my power. Compassion for yourself and others eases the disappointment of leaving comfortable places to join with others committed to full-hearted, life-long growth. This powerful synergy breaks the nets that ensnare you with messages saying that you don't deserve to live your dreams and should instead feed off someone else's leftovers.

> Compassion for yourself and others eases the disappointment of leaving comfortable places to join with others committed to full-hearted, life-long growth.

A client struggled to balance the "nets" of limiting messages with her inner belief she could run a successful, growing business. We examined the impact of her putting energy into trying to convince naysayers to accept her leadership style. As an exuberant woman of color, she unearthed a limiting message that she only had one chance to succeed so she had to do it perfectly. She also had to release the burden of feeling she was representing her race and gender.

THAT ONE THING... I understood from working with Linda that privilege does not exclude me from experiencing the limitations of oppression. I get to make best decision—not the perfect one—given the realities of societal stereotypes. I continually get data, change my situation to one that nurtures me more, and reap the benefits when I center my dreams. Most important, I use the privileges I have earned to be my full self and encourage others to do the same.

Sara Lawrence-Lightfoot, an author, educator, researcher, and public intellectual who blends art and science states: "What is fascinating—and disturbing—about most of the public discourse, policies, and educational practices is that there is seldom a reference to the longitudinal trajectory of learning across the life span." We must reject messages about urgency that makes us think time and opportunities have passed us by if we don't get it all together by a certain age. It is never too late to grow to your full size and it requires constant reflection and the support of a trusted tribe.

There are some typical glitches that can trap you and from which you can wiggle free. You can see big tunas as mythical creatures rather than as role models. You can also think that there is only one right way to be great or flourish rather than trusting your own style and path. This is especially likely if the big tunas in your field or area of passion do not look or sound like you, as role models are crucial for success and confidence. Another way to get tangled up in your "nets" is to be terrified of being a big tuna because of the social or familial isolation of being the "only one." As a formally educated, middle-class woman of color, I can be the only one in privileged settings. My protective survival mode is to get riled up about the ongoing lack of racial diversity in my yoga classes, at business conventions, and when river rafting. The problem is, starting from this place automatically shuts down my capacity to feel like I belong, and that then shuts down my capacity to be fully present and seek the gifts available to me. Over the years I have found ways to use my power to set up my best feeding grounds. A few strategies I use are to attend classes taught by BIPOC so I know I will not be alone, invite diverse friends on my outdoor adventures, and research event attendees ahead of time to intentionally connect with other underrepresented people.

Taking risks is indeed more challenging when you are breaking through an actual glass ceiling. What if, even amid the real hazards of finding your best feeding grounds, you expand your genuine happiness and fulfillment to balance the costs?

To grow to your full size, you first admit, without shame or blame, that you decided to play small. Not once, not twice, but as an unconscious, habitual survival practice in your life. Playing small looks different for everyone and can be true even if you have achieved financial or professional success by supporting someone else's dreams. This is where knowing and committing to your purpose matters.

Let me suggest a typical place we often do not make the effort to swim to and that we have a large amount of power to change: Physical health. Have you taken the time to decide what your optimal health is apart from the "one size fits all" formulas that can never work for everyone? Most people have a vague idea of an amount of exercise/movement, food, and drink parameters, along with a minimum sleep requirement. Have you researched what your body needs specific to your age, your preferences, and your lifestyle? Do you know what your body positively responds to? Are you diligent in honoring those needs, or do you follow a "one size fits all" approach because it seems easier than deciding and trusting your inner knowledge?

What is an initial mindset shift as you journey, mile by mile, to better feeding grounds? First, accept that you are exploring so you will make wrong turns or pick people or groups that don't support your growth. Use these as data to make future decisions rather than berating yourself. Oops, I got off at the wrong exit or trusted the wrong person to have my back. This is a good time to call a friend, reflect on lessons learned, and find your way back. Then scan for other options and make decisions that help you continue with grace and ease. There is plenty of room for an array of feelings and loving compassion. Layla Saad, author of *Me and White Supremacy*, anti-racism educator, international speaker, and podcast host, states: "Feeling the feelings—which are an appropriate human response to racism and oppression—is an important part of the process. When you allow yourself to feel those feelings, you wake up. You rehumanize yourself."

There is even room for growing in feeding grounds that are not ideal. In these circumstances I adjust my expectations and pace. As a competitive person, I used to be devastated when I lost anything, as I had no positive framework for understanding losing as a natural part of life. By fighting the insidious message that I was not expected to win as a woman and a person of color, my unconscious rage at that reality often "leaked" out inappropriately. I received my fair share of yellow cards on the soccer field and my (un)fair share of negative feedback in work situations where I spoke out against inequities. When I understood how much of my failure was based on external circumstances and power dynamics, I took the opportunity to assess both my responsibility and that of others, including institutions.

Losing in all its forms can contain wisdom, but so can winning, and the best wisdom is found in win-win situations (off the sports field!). If you are losing all the time and becoming bitter, then it's time to assess your feeding grounds, your mindset, and your support system. And when you win, don't brush it aside—pause to enjoy the moment.

The fable of Tunita shows us the value of perseverance and companionship. It is up to each of us to discover our dreams so that our inner Ferraris can rev up their motors. When you find your best feeding grounds, set yourself up to return to them regularly, regardless of the "nets" that will push you to settle. And if you are in a situation with a glass ceiling, find or create antidotes, places and people who support you through detours. Life is not a straight line. To grow to your full size means shifting to a fluid, circular, wave pattern approach that supports your health and well-being.

Ready for a #fullhearted breakthrough?
The messages I hear and/or have internalized that limit my growth are...
I am settling for okay instead of finding my best feeding grounds at...
The circumstances I flourish in are... (people, places, pace, ambiance)

Do it.
Tell someone who will hold you accountable your biggest, most audacious goal and one thing you will do to accomplish it.

7

Rest and Nest

What is easy is sustainable. Birds coast when they can.
— adrienne marie brown

REST. THE BODY NEEDS it to repair and replenish, the mind needs it to access reason and creativity, and the soul needs it to cultivate peace. When seals pull themselves out onto rocks or the shore, they are not being lazy or sunbathing. They haul out to reoxygenate their blood by sleeping much of the day. This and a thick layer of blubber enables them to take deep dives, staying underwater an average of twenty-three minutes as they forage, mostly at night, in the cold ocean waters off the coast. It is essential for them to rest. It saves their lives.

We too need to "reoxygenate." But unlike seals, we often forfeit our rest due to the "crisis" and "doing" paradigms of society. Rest is not seen as being productive.

As a self-employed entrepreneur and writer, much of my time is spent alone, the clock my guide or my punisher. This is further amplified because I am single, have no pets, and live alone. One might think that is the perfect set-up for rest, but it turns out it isn't.

While many people would envy my capacity to plan most of my time, there are downsides to not having a set schedule. I can minimize lunchtime and breaks, while some traditional work environments mandate these and others are full of colleagues who make time to chat or share lunch. A break for me can easily become house chores or a yoga class. Necessary parts of my life, but not true rest. While my pace is rarely rushed, my "doing" sometimes does not stop until I turn off the lights at night. (Even when in bed I am often reading, reflecting on my health, and reviewing the day for gratitudes.)

I became much more mindful of rest when a Buddhist teacher stated unambiguously that I was not sitting on my meditation cushion enough for someone with my practice history. My resistance, grounded in the impulse to "do", dissolved, and now regular meditation is a time where I watch my mind's frenetic activity with compassion and cultivate the power of nothing. While this is not physical rest, it can be a time to rest my mind. Being still when I want to get hooked into every thought that arises is practice that supports my rest off the cushion.

I am the queen of boundaries and accountability, and I have learned to apply those attributes to rest and rejuvenation. By debunking the idea that more effort is always better, I now create true rest times in my day. I sometimes watch my few favorite TV shows or sports to give myself a full meal break with no work.

Engaging, challenging work and other passions are not in opposition to rest—they work together. By committing to restful evenings and weekends, I then organize my work efficiently because I have a stop time. When I start flailing, I pull out a daily checklist I first developed thirty years ago as a gentle reminder to pay dedicated attention to my well-being. It now includes intentional rest habits—computer off earlier, forty-five-minute lunch break, in bed by 9–9:30, lights out by 10–10:30. I am grateful I can practice rest as conscientiously as I practice action.

Rest and self-care are recurring themes in my coaching practice, and I have coached many clients as they prepare to take a vacation. In their mind this is a time to relax, rejuvenate, and get away from the daily grind. To make this happen, they usually work extra hard in the weeks approaching their "time off" and do very little to ponder what they need to be doing before and during their vacation to assure they rest and rejuvenate.

Sound familiar? When your vacations fail to deliver, it's often because you do not invest the same level of thought and planning that you put into your "regular" life and your expectations are too high. In addition, it's easy to forget that other people make decisions that impact your precious vacation time—if you don't have a plan to counteract this.

Your work situation and other people in your life can hijack your mental space during vacation and eliminate any opportunity to rest. There was a rash of years when each of my vacations were undermined by the power dynamics in my workplace. While working as a supervisor for a county Child Welfare Services Division, I was involuntarily transferred to another location the day before my vacation. This was one of many signs that I would not receive the respect and value I desired. I left that job nine months later when I realized we were not helping black and brown families reunite, we were making sure they never would.

While going to the Masai Mara in Kenya and watching green turtles lay their eggs in Costa Rica were phenomenal to experience after each of these incidents, I did not return rejuvenated or rested. Pending work decisions distracted me from the magnificence of lions, waterfalls spilling over high cliffs, and lava flowing down a volcano.

Similarly, having twins a few years later discredited any remaining notion of a restful vacation when family and kids were involved. I freed myself from unrealistic expectations by calling these family trips. There might be some elements of rest involved, but these trips could be hectic as well, and shifting my expectations gave me the freedom to enjoy the restful moments in each trip and not feel frustrated.

I then recognized the short-sightedness of expecting a few days or weeks to replenish the drain of my ongoing life. The first step was clarifying for myself which activities (or nonactivities) truly led to the 4 "R"s as defined by Merriam-Webster:

Relaxation: relief from bodily and mental effort; diversion; entertainment

Rejuvenation: return to vigor

Restoration: make fresh or new again

Rest: refreshing quiet or repose of sleep; inactivity after exertion; relief and freedom from what wearies and disturbs; solitude; mental and spiritual calm; tranquility.

The whole idea that you need to vacate your life is both problematic and untenable. The goal then becomes making choices so you do not *want* to vacate your daily life. Start viewing healing, fun, and rest as integral parts of every day, not reserved for a magical vacation. Instead of dreaming of getting away from your life, notice each day when you want to leave emotionally or physically and examine why. Then determine what actions to take to center you in that moment, based on what is possible. A few deep breaths can calm your nervous system and send oxygen to your brain so you can reflect on your wish to vacate with curiosity and compassion.

Much of what wearies us are nicks, subtle aggressions, and repetitive power plays that we manage well in the moment while forgetting the cumulative effect will catch up with us. Eventually, our emotional blood sugar crashes and we do something that is not skillful and leads to negative consequences rather than an examination of structural oppression. Figure out how you can, little by little, notice the urges to leave a moment and stay long enough to consider which healthy options are available to tend to your fatigue.

One of my clients asked for assistance in integrating healthy ways to release stress. We first worked to shift her stated belief that she had to be busy to be productive, which excluded social relationships like her family, partner, colleagues, and friends. She had also presumed that having many BIPOC in her department would feel supportive, forgetting positional and gender dynamics would be in play.

THAT ONE THING… I came to see through my work with Linda how I gave up my freedom, joy, and self-care for external attention at work. I then committed to meeting my needs in a healthy way by exploring what worked for me. By having internally-driven options, I could release my worry of doing it right.

When your computer or phone battery is low, you don't hesitate to plug them in. When putting fuel in the tank of your car or charging its electric battery, you don't think "this is taking away from my driving." What are signs your emotional, spiritual and/or physical batteries are running low? Practice no hesitation when you need to refuel your mind, body, and spirit.

You can increase your level of rejuvenation and rest with one-to-ten-minute activities that fit into any day, no matter how busy: meditation, deep breathing, silence, nature, music, dancing, or closing your eyes, to name a few. What recharges your batteries? Each person will answer this differently. If you don't know what re-fuels you and prioritize these throughout your day, your time will be subsumed by other people's needs, by media, and by old unhealthy habits. Not committing to rest will inevitably lead to distractions that ease anxiety and fear temporarily rather than contributing to the process of thriving. Note when you are zoning out versus engaging in genuine rest. This places higher expectations on your vacations and weekends and offers less and less ease in the life you lead 95 percent of the time. Focus on filling that 95 percent of your life with rest opportunities and watch the magic happen.

> Focus on filling that 95 percent of your life with rest opportunities and watch the magic happen.

Define for yourself what your favorite vacation elements are and explore how to make them daily, weekly, monthly, and yearly practices. Will you fall off your practices? You bet. I fall off all the time, but my habits are always a few pages of a good book or hot cup of tea away. Incorporate your essential elements into a daily checklist and put the elements that are weekly or monthly into your planning tools. Do the same with yearly practices—family, partner, and/or solo dates and trips, travel to places within an hour that rejuvenate you, and enjoyable activities. Your checklist is not linear and not a rigid mandate; it is a barometer that allows you to move with your internal beat.

The most important of all of these are your everyday practices, which hold the highest possibility of rest. Studies show the profound value of deep breathing, sleep, hourly breaks, movement, healthy foods (the ones that are right for *your* body), and hydration.

Heart disease, stroke, and diabetes are diseases related to stress that are killing black women at an alarming rate—connected to the stress of persistent, daily racism and sexism. According to the U.S. Department of Health and Human Services, "Latinas have high rates of factors that increase the risk of developing heart disease, such as diabetes, obesity, and physical inactivity, while heart disease accounts for a third of all deaths among Latinas." You cannot stop these attacks on your well-being, but you can control many aspects of your health. Do you feel bad when you are sick? The root is perfectionism and the false narrative that women, BIPOC, and others with less access to resources can do it all even as we carry a heavier load because of oppression. That makes no sense. It also re-enforces the Western model of separation of body, mind, and spirit. We know each of these aspects is connected to the others, which is why nourishing any nourishes them all.

Still, committing to rest and self-care requires a wakeful attitude. Is it more helpful to skip a workout and instead stretch to tend to your sore muscles or broken heart? Is nutritional cleansing a better option than eating so your organs can rest and do their internal replenishing?

A client told me her cheesy pleasure was listening to a ballad by Journey and singing along at the top of her lungs in the car. I am a loud song with windows open person myself, sometimes with tears streaming down my face. Allow yourself these free form moments when judgment slips away. Without enough rest, it's easy to resist the tasks with the potential to create the breakthroughs you seek, the ones that can give you the life you deserve. Be as ambitious and accountable with rest as you are with your other goals.

> Be as ambitious and accountable with rest as you are with your other goals.

One of my clients was preparing for a large work event where her usual pattern was to work many hours, take care of others, and ignore self-care and rest. I asked her to be willing to do it differently and see herself as modeling leadership that championed self-care for her team of mostly women of color. She created a visual of the schedule and marked self-care opportunities for herself to interrupt her pattern of taking care of others to her detriment. I pointed out the subtle ways she slipped into white supremacy behaviors like paternalism, individualism, and one right way. She acknowledged the downside of exhausting herself: she didn't bring her best self to the situation. I invited her to be transparent with her team about the negative consequences of her being below capacity. She set limits on what she could do at work apart from the tasks associated with this special event. She had a breakthrough and saw that nothing bad would happen if she and her co-director, also a woman of color, took a week off after the event as did the rest of the team. She came to understand that her overwork and over-caregiving was compelled by a need to prove she deserved to be a leader.

This is an example of a client who made a big move to support her rest and self-care and be a model for her team. But these practices can be small. One of my simplest rest practices is having water within arm's reach throughout the day. The act of drinking means I am hydrated and stop often to use the bathroom, a built-in moment of rest and movement. This often leads me to scan my environment and seek beauty, usually focusing on nature—the sky, plants, sunshine. Sometimes it is art, music, pictures of those I love, or yes, even my own reflection in the mirror.

Ready for a #fullhearted breakthrough?

For my home to encourage me to rest easily I will…

Signs my internal battery is in the red are…

Easily accessible sources of fuel that fill my emotional and spiritual tank are…

Do it.

Plan rest activities today and put in your calendar.

8

Love Yourself Well

The real thing that we renounce is the tenacious hope
that we could be saved from being who we are.
—Pema Chödrön

L OVING YOURSELF WELL IS a fundamental act in supporting
your well-being. It requires believing that you do not need to
be saved from being yourself. You chose to be who you are. We are
born with a belief in our worthiness—as babies and little children we
insisted on the value of our needs and the right to have them met.

Slowly, we were hit with adultism, the societally enforced norm
that gives adults the right to control children above and beyond
making sure we do not come to or create harm. This is a reality
rarely acknowledged or discussed. We have it bred into our souls—
like a hazing process that we then turn around and inflict on others.
Think about how you behave when you enter a group with adults
and children. I know I have ingested the belief I can ignore them and
simply introduce myself to the adults with few negative repercussions.
Do you insist they act like mini-adults rather than consider an age-
appropriate greeting? What if children received the basic respect
of feeling seen by our words and actions? I have committed to

acknowledging and greeting every child and young person I meet in a manner that is comfortable for them. bell hooks, an author, professor, feminist, and social activist states: "when we love children we acknowledge by our every action that they are not property, that they have rights—that we respect and uphold their rights."

Because most of us have internalized that children are less important that adults—we have set the foundation for the better than/less than paradigm that underlies all oppression. When we are treated poorly by people with structurally supported power, it triggers the lessons we were taught as children about our value. With that as a backdrop, you shouldn't be surprised at how poorly you may still treat yourself or how often you feel others are treating you "like a child." When you add in societal mandates that value white supremacy, you can understand it was not your conscious decision to feel diminished.

To love yourself well amid constant and historical personal and communal trauma, look for signs of your immense heart, mind, and spirit. First and foremost, notice what is available in each moment to supports your friendship with yourself. (I developed the habit of kissing myself, especially on the top of my shoulder, when I am in bed. It is a sweet and simple way to remember that I am my best friend, no matter what occurs.) During the day, look for the ways the world "kisses" you—the scent of a candle, a "like" on your social media, or a song that makes your body move. Notice when you seek affirmation from people who can't celebrate you because of jealousy or a scarcity mentality that only one of you gets to shine.

To shift internalized messages you may have received about being unlovable, examine the foundations of your life. Find the comments in the past that negated your self-love, and take the time to consciously reject them now as an adult: *Children are to be seen and not heard, Because I said so, Your attitude is too uppity or You are stupid—a burra.* With that work begun, breathe in early truths that were stifled, when you knew without a doubt you were worthy. Say now, with adult power and wisdom: "I respect and value my needs. There is enough for me and others to be loved."

One of the most profound healing processes I learned from Visions, Inc.[2] trainings is that there are no good or bad feelings; they are messengers that signal what we want or need, which is especially crucial in cross-cultural interactions. Acknowledge and listen to the messages your feelings give you. When something hurts, it hurts, regardless of intention. When you are mad, set or reset expectations and boundaries. When you cry, find the source of sadness and grieve. When you laugh, enjoy the delight fully. When you are afraid, seek protection and support. When you feel strong, act thoughtfully. Your capacity to love is developed from the inside out and continues your entire life.

> Your capacity to love is developed from the inside out and continues your entire life.

Sometimes loyalty can get in the way of loving ourselves well. I have been loyal to people and organizations to my detriment—trying too hard and for too long to be seen and have my gifts utilized. I am now loyal to my values and my purpose first. If a person or organization allows you to contribute your talents and receive respect and grow, then that is the time to be all in. If not, no amount of effort will suffice and you can instead shift your energy to seeking a nurturing environment.

Another challenge to loving yourself well is only giving to others instead of being kind and generous to yourself. When you don't include yourself in loving acts, it can twist your relationships into a "tit for tat" dynamic. You can be unconscious of your expectations of others to reciprocate and the strings you attach. "See how I do this for you? Do it for me." You may never say this, but it is your primordial plea, your belief that others' love is the key to your worthiness—that it is out of your hands. This is particularly true for women, as we are still socially conditioned and institutionally mandated to take care of others first. For BIPOC, we are conditioned to accede to white people's right to comfort, a subtle, unloving white supremacy behavior. Instead of being only focused on other people's needs and approval, you can choose to include yourself in the healing

---

[2]   Visions-inc.org

you possess. Being your own best friend means constantly tending to yourselves so you can live with an open heart, mind, and spirit.

I have worked with many clients whose purpose is to support BIPOC, immigrants, LGBTQ+ communities, and families who are most negatively impacted by current policies and laws. One client who ran programs to develop leadership for women of color said taking care of herself was "indulgent", which led her to repeatedly ignore her needs. The negative impacts of not loving herself well included her illnesses, her resentment towards those for whom she provided services, and her estrangement from friends who she never made time to see. She ultimately committed to framing self-love as what she required to stay healthy, happy, and generous. I had another client who was the oldest daughter in a family of immigrants, regularly taking care of her younger siblings and sending money to her mother. She expressed her worry about being "irresponsible" by seeking support for herself. I smiled and told her, as I have told many clients, that not doing enough would never be her issue. Her issue was not consistently attending to her well-being and the example she was setting for others like herself to ignore their needs.

A dedicated commitment to loving ourselves means learning to manage culturally-sponsored addictive behaviors that lead to disregarding ourselves. One habit to we will break again and again is comparing ourselves with people who live with simpler agendas, more support, and generational privilege. Take stock of differences that either give or limit ease in loving yourself well. Commit to adjusting your expectations and your pace when the terrain is rough due to work inequities, family crises, and/or personal growth spurts. When the road is flatter, notice that too and speed up, but not so fast that you don't enjoy the journey, because it *is* the destination.

Loving yourself well is acknowledging that you can find ways to thrive amid ongoing waves of injustice. Learning about horrible news from others in your life and from the larger communities around you, sometimes called vicarious trauma, is important to factor into what you can commit to at any given moment. Monnica Williams, a psychologist, professor, and director of the University of Louisville's

Center for Mental Health Disparities, stated in an interview with Jenna Wortham of the *New York Times*: "Because the African-American community has such a long history of pervasive discrimination, something that impacts someone miles away can sometimes impact all of us. That's what I mean by vicarious traumatization." That is what spurs the Black Lives Matter movement.

You can balance this difficult stress with the positive stress of doing what you love. Sometimes I choose to go to a social justice rally or write to someone in an ICE detention facility, and sometimes I choose to write, play tennis, or sleep longer. The tendency is to do less self-care when your communities are attacked, but you must do the same amount or more. Otherwise you will be doing what you are fighting to end—harm to yourself and others. By becoming the beloved recipient of your own generosity and kindness, you heal your wounds fully and open possibilities for yourself and for the generations to come.

I worked with a client who was committed to others' care to the detriment of her own needs. She had to break through her belief that loving herself was not a leadership quality and see how it fortified her to do better for herself and her staff.

THAT ONE THING... I was considering how to respond to a staff member who was struggling around white allyship, and Linda reminded me that it wasn't my job to rescue her or make her feel better. That as a leader, it was my job to set boundaries and that setting boundaries is the compassionate thing to do because that lays the groundwork for healthy cultural norms for all.

One client became aware that loving herself allowed her to not know everything. She was instead establishing new loving habits of acknowledging her feelings to herself: *I've had a really hard day— what can I do to replenish?* and *I love how I sat with my discomfort even as challenges tried to knock me off my path.*

I had a client who interviewed to be an Executive Director and was told by the interviewing committee that they wanted to hire a man since non-profits are "dominated" by women. It is important to distinguish between the numerical majority and the power majority. While more than 75 percent of the non-profit workforce is women, just 18 percent have a female CEO, and women of color are even less represented. My client struggled through the antagonistic interview and called the recruiter afterwards, angrily telling him she should never have been sent to that interview, as they did not value her as a woman of color. We discussed her valid rage and how to maintain a neutral stance in a situation where you are not seen and appreciated: "Ah, this is happening." Slow breath. Decide how to stay true to your best self. Sometimes it means saying something, like when I told my male tennis partner to ask permission before offering me advice on my game. Sometimes it means staying silent and getting support elsewhere, like when I overheard a woman in my workout group comment how grateful the "Mexican girl" was when she received the woman's used clothing, never noticing she just worked out next to a Latina. Many of you are like the canary in the mine—the first to feel the danger because you are the one *in* the most danger. Notice and remember the triggers that tell you danger is in the air so you can act to save who you really are, not what people want you to be. Loving yourself is a daily practice that is rooted in knowing we do not have to be saved from being who we are—keep your head up and your heart forward to guide you.

Ready for a #fullhearted breakthrough?

Find a picture of yourself as a child where you see your joy and sense of worthiness shining. (If you can't, then find one of a child you love who can be your guiding star.)

What I knew then was…

The gifts I have to offer are…

I stay true to my best self by…

Do it.

Do two things today to love yourself.

Section 3

Consistent, Authentic Confidence

9

Trust Your Heart

> Because one believes in oneself, one doesn't try to
> convince others. Because one is content with oneself,
> one doesn't need others' approval.
>
> —Lao Tzu

CONFIDENCE IS SOMETHING MY friends and clients seem to consider more a mystery than a characteristic they draw on easily in their lives. To develop and maintain a strong, authentic confidence, you must be able to rely mostly on *self-generated* confidence. Merriam-Webster defines confidence as "a feeling or consciousness of one's powers; a visceral belief that one will act well; a relation of trust or intimacy." While Merriam-Webster means the last aspect to be between two people, I suggest you consider how to do this with yourself. To possess self-generated confidence, you must relate intimately with and trust your inner voice; including forgiving yourself when you're overwhelmed by what's expected of you. Many of my clients discuss the emotional labor required of them particularly as women of color who are expected to tend to the feelings of other BIPOC and of white staff and board.

Authentic, full-hearted confidence is the opposite of perfectionism or certainty. It does not ascribe to the "fake it till you make it" model, which is a narrative that primarily works when there are safety nets to catch you like gender, race, and/or class privileges. A more genuine mantra is "I trust my experience and resilience and take strategic risks."

> Authentic, full-hearted confidence is the opposite of perfectionism or certainty.

What does self-generated confidence look like in action? I worked with a client who was fired from his position on the leadership team at a corporate firm and requested assistance in increasing his diminished confidence. He was the only person of color on the management team in a company that was doing poorly. In only firing him, the CEO's excuse was that my client hadn't solved a few problems, even though he had no authority or responsibility in the relevant area, a sales and marketing department that was leaking profits—and which was headed by white men. He was determined to cultivate a resilient confidence that bent but did not break under duress. Self-generated confidence surfaced as the missing element in his life, especially because externally generated confidence was out of his sphere of influence, even with his high level of education and heretofore stellar work history. By unconsciously depending too much on the accolades, raises, and promotions of his past, he had set the stage for this situation as a moment of deep and painful reflection.

I asked this client to notice and document negative thoughts *and* their origins in our first weeks of working together. Some thoughts he unburied were: *A thousand people standing behind me can do this job* and *If I was strong enough, I wouldn't need help.* He had learned confidence-eroding thoughts from his family, community, and society that had become unconsciously embedded in his mind and heart. He was compelled now to pay attention to how these kinds of negative thoughts were tied to his lack of societal power as an African American and reinforced a system of better than/less than.

My client's most powerful disempowering thought emerged as we continued to work together: *If I was truly great, they wouldn't have been able to let me go.* I gently pointed out that he was on the Titanic and no matter how well he met his goals, he was not going to get a seat on the lifeboat. He had neither the right skin color nor the relational power with the CEO, who told my client he wanted to be surrounded by people he was comfortable with during the crisis.

When I read an article that stated: "Women applied for a promotion only when they met 100 percent of the qualifications. Men applied when they met 50 percent"— I noticed that these statistics were not broken down by race. The author, a white woman, framed the issue as a lack of confidence and said nothing about the relentless sexism, racism, and the added inequities women of color face in the workplace. If the author had explored the impact of race, she might have found women of color don't even apply when they are 100 percent qualified, often because their outcomes have been so bleak. The 2020 Race to Lead Revisited report affirmed their earlier 2017 report findings that women of color reported being passed over for new jobs or promotions in favor of men of color, white women, and white men with comparable or even lower credentials.[3]

Rather than understanding the impact of race *and* gender, white women focus on where they experience inequities. Society's white narrative tells them they should be successful. As women they feel the inequities and blame themselves or sexism rather than seeing the duality of also having white privilege. Since they have far more access than BIPOC to frame issues, they continue a deficit-based, white supremacy analysis. This mentality is used constantly—a lack of housing, educational access, promotional opportunities, healthy food, and clean water to name some prevalent ones. There is no lack of confidence or of anything else, there is an inequitable distribution of resources by people in power who control decision-making.

The effect of multiple power inequities must be part of your analysis of your level of confidence—you can't depend on others to

---

3   https://buildingmovement.org/reports/race-to-lead-revisited-national-report/

do this. For example, by both race and gender, a higher percentage of black women are enrolled in college than any other group. Yet black women make up just 8 percent of private sector jobs and 1.5 percent of leadership roles. Authentic confidence is not resolved when women of color apply for jobs for which they are 50 percent qualified when both racism and sexism exist. The Race to Lead data confirms what my clients and I have experienced for decades—to "lean in" someone has to "lean forward" to meet you. Otherwise no amount of extra effort and "male-like" behavior will close the gap and you end up in a faceplant, blaming your lack of confidence.

Years ago, in looking at how generational internalized oppression works, I saw how I had bought into negative thoughts as a woman of color with immigrant parents who did their best to fit in. My parents wanted me to succeed and I watched their deferential behavior with white people outside the home, signaling to me I had to tone down my exuberant personality. They never spoke of their struggles so I harbored the false notion that I could overcome inequities by learning and following the rules. In some ways I am glad my creative indignant nature couldn't abide the injustices I saw and experienced. While that led to negative repercussions, it also led me to search for a different paradigm where I was not always the "wrong" one. In my work with social justice, feminist, and spiritual groups, I slowly understood that being a formally educated, English-fluent US citizen did not eliminate oppression. The most important lesson I learned was to identify thoughts that made me the problem, especially those that started with the words: *I should have.* Those words put an expectation on me to know and anticipate white supremacy culture as well as live by its characteristics of perfectionism and one right way.

This internalization of myself as "less than" started as a child, something that became obvious to me when I read the journal I kept from age eleven to sixteen. It was full of comments that put a positive spin on blue eyes, straight hair, and downplaying my intelligence while disparaging my appearance and personality. I read through it to save a few parts as memorabilia, but decided instead to recycle the whole thing, releasing the self-hate I had learned and practiced for years towards myself, and by extension, towards people like me.

The Toltecs say there is a "mitote" in your mind that keeps you from your truest, freest self. This mitote sounds like 1,000 people talking and nobody listening. In your mind it is the judge and the victim, as well as voices that attack, defend, and justify your actions, fears, loves, masks, and strategies. Don Miguel Ruiz, a renowned spiritual teacher and international bestselling author, discusses this thoroughly in *The Four Agreements*. The voice of mitote is quelled by strengthening your nurturing, wise voice. This means developing antidotes to your negative thoughts and remembering it is a constant, life-long practice to trust your heart. There is no end to the rage, there are only healthy strategies and a community to uplift you when you fall.

I always have my clients develop a vision of what they will be feeling, thinking, and doing in a year. This exercise is designed to identify and counteract negative thoughts that undercut self-generated confidence. It is not a broad *you can do this* affirmation. I encourage specificity and a focus only on what my clients can influence—their own feelings, thoughts, and behaviors. One of the comments I often add to their drafts of their vision is, "You can't *make* people trust or respect you. What are skills or actions you are committed to developing?"

In reviewing the vision of the client who was let go of his corporate job, I encouraged him to include developing his self-generated voice of confidence. Once he recognized his nurturing voice as the one he used with his son, it became easier for him to use this voice with himself because he saw the benefit. My client then consciously assessed which attitudes he had inherited from his family that he would discard and which ones he wanted to pass on to his son to build his confidence. Breaking our patterns allows us to positively influence ourselves and those we love rather than try endlessly to prove we are good enough.

I use my inner nurturing voice daily, the product of years of practice. When I miss an overhead at tennis practice, I mentally note what I did right before thinking about how to correct what I did wrong. I remind myself to hit the ball in front of me rather than saying what I hear from the women around me: *I am so stupid* or *How could I...*fill in the blank. Given the strength and reinforcement of the mitote voice reinforced by society, I self-correct constantly.

Be rigorous so that the winds of life do not topple your self-generated confidence: Make time every day to listen to and heed your nurturing voice. I end each day expressing gratitudes and always make sure to appreciate myself first.

Another important aspect of confidence is noticing any patterns you may have around deflecting compliments or feeling you need to say something positive back. These behaviors are steeped in a discomfort with praise and in wanting to be liked. "Thank you" is enough. Your inner wisdom will let you know when the praise is coming from someone else's lack of confidence or their wish to affirm only aspects of you that match theirs. If the compliment is genuine, take it in completely. If not, then "thank you" is the appropriate response to close the conversation and not get trapped trying to make them feel better.

Self-generated confidence is a practice with valuable repercussions. Apart from feeling surer of yourself and able to accept compliments from others, it performs another significant task. It allows you to weigh external evaluation against data from your own truth. After a training, presentation, or performance, I evaluate myself first, so that other feedback is assessed based on my inner wisdom. I delineate what I did well, especially given challenging circumstances, and note one or two things I would have done differently. This pride, dipped in a warm coating of humility and joy, counteracts any feedback that comes from people's biases.

This showed up with a client who spent too much time relying on external feedback for her sense of confidence rather than developing self-appreciation. I encouraged her to keep her focus on her vision and goals when evaluating her behavior.

THAT ONE THING... Linda has really helped me set healthy goals as a woman of color leader. Her gentle but firm reminders that I can't control other people's behavior shifted my focus to set goals on how I want to show up. I developed my own barometer for measuring my performance, rather than basing it on how others perceive it.

It is nearly impossible to not want and overprize others' approval, especially in a society that constantly tells you that you are less valuable or important than others based on status. However, when you feel the desperate edge of needing that approval, it is a sign to cultivate your inner wisdom and get back to basic self-care—rest, pleasurable activities, and time with your tribe of loving, generous people. James Baldwin summed up the importance of self-generated confidence: "The place in which I'll fit will not exist until I make it."

By increasing your ability to give generously and honestly to yourself and accept positive regard, you can then give it to others freely—without needing to convince them—from a place of detachment and abundance.

Ready for a #fullhearted breakthrough?
The loudest mitote thought I will create an antidote for is…
People who give me genuine compliments are…
One thing I can do to increase my self-generated confidence is….

Do it.
Eliminate the phrase "lack of" and see what you can say instead.

10
Be 100 Percent

It takes tremendous discipline, takes tremendous courage, to think for yourself, to examine yourself.

—Cornel West

FOR "125-PERCENT" PEOPLE, GIVING enough isn't the problem. Do you know someone like this? Are you this person? These "125" percenters give beyond what is needed and beyond what is healthy for their body, mind, and spirit. One of their characteristics is an overemphasis on external praise rather than internal confidence. Another key characteristic is a fear, even more pronounced in BIPOC, of being an imposter—that is, someone who is not what they say they are. My clients often struggle to believe they have the right to be in positions of power or succeed because they have so few role models. They then try to be perfect.

Society throws around the word *overwork* in a "one size fits all" manner, not noting that the reasons people engage in that behavior can be profoundly different for those who must prove themselves constantly because of biases. When your competence is not given credence or you don't get the necessary resources to succeed, your internalized glass ceiling says you cannot fail (and will not be given a second chance if you do). This feeds the push to do more than 100 percent, and the long-term cost of internalized doubt and perfectionism can show up both physically and emotionally.

Even with years of awareness, I still catch a thought in my head that grinds my joy to dust: *If I had just said it perfectly, I wouldn't feel uncomfortable.* These moments happen when I am saying something that challenges a person or group's perspective, especially around race or another power dynamic. I deserve to have my truth matter and be listened to carefully. When someone instead disagrees with no room for a different opinion, I get stuck in thinking I could have been stronger or kinder or louder or quieter. It is a defense mechanism to protect myself from rage, grief, and/or fear and I am never surprised when this pattern emerges with my clients.

I listen for the extra 25 percent thoughts from my clients to help them recognize their internalized perfectionism, which is different than having high standards. Identifying the behaviors of white supremacy allow you to, with a relaxed approach, reject them with a more grounded thought: Because I took a risk and spoke my truth as skillfully as I could, I am on the edge of growth, which always feels scary/uncomfortable. Why? Because you are committed to releasing patterns and thoughts that no longer, if ever, served you.

Another thing that propels 125 percent behavior is the notion that if you do more, you can save people. This is particularly embedded in BIPOC and immigrants who have a level of social class and formal education denied to their parents and communities. These people take on financial and emotional obligations that place pressure on them to work more. One client said: "I have always been the 'shield', taking the biggest blows for others."

I told her to remember she often entered situations well into the cycle of historical injustice. Another client said about a family member who kept asking for her help: "I don't want to wreck her by not responding." I kindly reminded her she could not fix or be the tipping point for damage done over twenty years. When BIPOC and women have socially and economically prescribed roles as caretakers and their paid work is centered in social justice, being overwhelmed can be inevitable. This feeds the sense of not being good enough when the issue is you are simply exhausted from so many years of doing more than your body, mind, and spirit should bear. It is not enough to take off some of the load that is not yours and think the work is done. Another load is always waiting. Even in a moment of fighting against police brutality and historical anti–Blackness, I had to caution women of color to stop organizing resources to share with white people, who have always had the resources to educate themselves if they wanted.

To eliminate that 25 percent of added baggage, expand the image of yourself beyond being predominantly a helper and advocate. To do so requires a firm commitment to recognizing and admitting when and how have you unnecessarily rescued people by patching holes, hinting rather than speaking plainly, and taking on responsibilities so quickly they couldn't. When you rely on feeling needed for a false sense of power, it supports no one's well-being.

I worked with a writer who had decided to leave her job as a Program Director so she could pursue her MFA in writing. Instead of being proud about her decision, she worried about how to tell the agency she was leaving. She not only gave them four months' notice, she also offered to create a transition plan and lead the search process for her replacement. She told herself she was doing this for the under-resourced, predominantly immigrant students and families. Underneath this layer of presumed generosity, she was still proving her worth by making everything easy for everyone else, motivated by that external pull for praise. There was also some quiet guilt that she was leaving for her own joy. Much of what drove her to tie her self-worth to what she could do for people stemmed from her childhood as the oldest daughter of immigrants. Some beliefs from her that confirmed this were: *If I do things right, I will save my family* and *Pretty, fun, and social aren't going to get me anything.*

This "either/or thinking" of white supremacy leads people to see the choice as giving more or failing. Since failure is not an option if you are to save your family or your client or your partner, the only option is trying harder; giving to others in a way that's hard to stop or even control. The great thing about understanding this push, as she did, is that you can then break through the either/or internal paradigm. She finally put some effort into figuring out how she could make things easier for herself. The tool I suggested to her was practicing having her exit activities be "good enough." She then used her creativity to explore more easeful options based on abundance rather choosing between failure and giving more. Once she believed she had more options, that took care of the worry of doing it "the right way."

We worked on her doing as little as possible for the last month, since she had already done far more than most people do when leaving their jobs. Scaling back gave her the emotional energy to be present with the rainbow of feelings she experienced in leaving her job—the loss of relationships, the joy of a new beginning, and the disappointment of the organization's leadership to accomplish more.

"Good enough" might be poor advice for people in other situations, but for 125 percent people, it is simply pulling back to 100 percent. Every one of those percentage points can feel like cloud cover dispersing so you see and appreciate each moment. You can then direct energy toward your needs in a healthy way. Another aspect of that 25 percent is that over-efforting makes your light too bright, and people know it is not genuine. They then pull away. Being 100 percent means being yourself without pretense. It requires infinite trust in yourself—which doesn't mean you never "overdo it." It just means that you catch yourself sooner and sooner, recognizing when you're doing so out of fear that you're not enough.

There are other reasons why my clients take on that excess 25 percent. Some are used to "winging it," as they have not had the privilege to be mentored, trained, or formally supported, and are trying to catch up. This is problematic because it presumes your effort can overcome historical and current glass ceilings. Others are reenacting childhood patterns of being in situations with no healthy adult around and handling everything by themselves. Finally, others unconsciously think they can change people—and the current effects of historical oppression—by doing more, inadvertently absorbing negative energy in the process.

Eliminating the "either/or" dichotomy allows you to move from an individualistic, isolated approach to being transparent with people you trust about what is hindering your progress, even if your organization does not model this. While you may understand the importance of teamwork when you are on a project, you may fail to apply this to your work and personal life. The message that an accomplished person can make quick decisions and figure out any challenge alone is rampant. I used to try to figure out everything by myself and now eliminate my frustration by asking for support from someone who has the knowledge base I don't. In reality, very little must be decided alone, especially with technology that allows us to connect across time zones and via multiple platforms. I have clients who cancel our sessions because they are "overwhelmed" or because they want to figure some things out before we speak. I remind them that isolation is the cornerstone of oppression, and that when they are struggling it is exactly the right moment for a session.

BIPOC also take on the added 25 percent when they are the only one in an environment and are expected to represent their race or communities. This unfair burden often causes anxiety—speak up and at least share some accurate information out, stay silent and allow people to stay uninformed, or call out people for this false narrative. Many of my clients are also expected to initiate discussions on equity when it is not in their specific job description and the organization espouses it as a value, which means it should be everyone's work.

A final aspect of why BIPOC and women work 25 percent more is the ongoing wage gap. Working harder is a necessary economic strategy to earn what you deserve for the same work. The key is to recognize when this is not true and when you're simply overworking out of habit or fear.

> *Being 100 percent means following the spirit of your commitments and not getting too caught in the exactitude of the how and the when.*

Being 100 percent means following the spirit of your commitments and not getting too caught in the exactitude of the how and the when. I often tell my clients they can often learn more when they don't comply with the commitments they made. It can highlight that they have the wrong goals or that they failed to consider what might derail them. One client's coping mechanism was to keep her goals small, not acknowledging what she really wanted so that she didn't feel bad when she didn't get it. You are allowed and encouraged to have high expectations of yourself based on an accurate assessment of your circumstances. It means being comfortable—while not always overjoyed—with not knowing. Repeated failure is the path to reaching your best if you pause to learn the lessons. It is not proof you cannot achieve your aspirations.

One of my clients is a poet who struggled to understand how to measure her work and words, feeling caught in the dominant paradigm of success. She felt pressure to do more than was possible given the publishing industry's track record of not valuing diverse voices.

THAT ONE THING... Linda is a fellow writer, a coach, and a woman of wisdom. She told me: "We don't necessarily have a sense of our influence on others for much of our lives. Can we measure the reach of a book in terms of how much it touches someone vs. how many people have read or bought the book? Yes, we can."

This thought remained with me through the process of releasing my first book. I have really enjoyed focusing on the depth with which a word or a line percolated with a reader. This is dialogue. It is connection. It makes for far more meaning than sales and breadth of distribution. Linda's words released me from some superficial obligations.

I have heard tennis commentators say: "She just doesn't feel nerves." As I see it, they are affirming a better than/less than paradigm that insists we can eliminate a natural response to stress. Every tennis player—and every person—feels nerves, anxiety, and fear. The work is to both listen to your feelings and engage your thoughts in guiding your actions. The key is to remember you are never fully alone—in those times when you don't achieve what you wanted, there are people who have gone before you, people going with you on a parallel path, and others watching so they can learn. This is true in success as well.

Sometimes I think: *This is not ideal, not ideal at all.* Then the voice of mercy responds with one of my antidotes to perfectionism: "That'll do, little pig, that'll do." This was spoken by the guardian of Babe, the little pig that did good enough to achieve his best in the movie *Babe*. "Good enough" means doing our best in each moment—but no more than we need to—and is what leads to uncomplicated joy and 100 percent living. By examining your 25 percent patterns, you can enjoy the power of less.

The best metaphor for living a 100 percent life is imagining each relationship with a person as a bridge. You are responsible to get to the middle of the bridge. The other person's task is to meet you there. The 25 percent urge arises when you are alone and think if you just take a few more steps, the other person will come and engage. The question to ask is whether that is what you want—to always be the one making the extra effort. I had to decide consciously that I want to be on bridges where I met the person, organization, or family member in the middle in a mutually beneficial, caring connection. The middle is not a rigid line and does not mean we all do the same thing. It means that we believe and act from a place of abundance—there is enough for all. It could be useful to map out both your most balanced and most unbalanced relationships to decide how you could shift where you are on each bridge. If you are over-efforting on several bridges, you are likely not getting to the middle of other bridges with people who can engage you in bountiful ways.

When you take away the excess 25 percent, you free up bandwidth for a different kind of "doing", like taking the game-changing steps to get where you want to go, or more "being" activities to care for yourself and therefore for others. Instead of trying to prove themselves to people who will never see their value, my clients connect with people who can mentor them or help them find another work opportunity. They also embrace joy-producing activities like dance, hikes, and sleeping enough so they are truly rested. This is the real bonus of living a courageous 100 percent life.

Ready for a #fullhearted breakthrough?
My excess 25 percent comes from old patterns that say...
A few steps to make 100 percent a reality would be...
What I will do with my added bandwidth is...

Do it.
Get off a task/project/board/committee that is draining your spirit.

11
Focus on Inner Wisdom

> Praise and blame, gain and loss, pleasure and sorrow
> come and go like the wind. To be happy, rest like a
> giant tree in the midst of them all.
>
> —Buddha

WHAT ARE YOU WITHOUT the bells and whistles, without the covers and cloaks society insists are necessary so you can be accepted by the status quo? When you turn from the glare of external pressures, what lies inside is your inner wisdom.

You know that voice, the one that is gentle, prodding, loving. The one that believes in your joy and prosperity. The voice that gets drowned out by internalized naysayers that surface when you are tired, have suffered multiple aggressions, and cannot hold on to your sense of self-worth and your accomplishments. This voice reminds you not to allow a world of injustice and sorrow to trash your precious gifts. *I know you*, says the voice. *I see you fully and I appreciate you.*

Trusting and sharing your wisdom means first creating space for it to settle in your bones. An example: A client felt disheartened in a hostile work environment, one where the director was known for pushing out black women and silencing them with a non-disclosure agreement tied to their severance package. I reminded my client she had already made things happen because of trusting her inner wisdom and sharing a vision connected to the goals the organization said were vital. To combat the racism, I encouraged her to stop scrambling to stay ahead of a game she would inevitably lose and instead look for another work option. I don't say this lightly and it is never because my clients aren't able to fulfill and even exceed their work requirements. However, not acknowledging external glass ceilings makes it difficult to avoid internalizing them.

In these environments, focusing on your inner wisdom is both more challenging and more necessary. At its core, it is as simple as trusting what you know and believe. No hesitation, no second thoughts. You tell yourself: *I will not doubt my inner voice.*

Living from an internal compass has a cost when you face inequities every day. As another client began to speak her truth in her office, she received negative feedback for not being "nicer" without them explicitly adding: "to white people." She felt hurt and told me: "I am so sensitive," which came from thinking she could be bigger than the structural racism in her organization. I encouraged her to frame the discouragement she felt as her skill of empathy. She easily absorbed the energy of those around her and it depleted her capacity to listen to her inner wisdom, along with her notion that she was "a fixer." If she chose to speak her truth about the power dynamics in her allegedly equity-oriented workplace, she had to shield herself. Why? You can't out-white, out-male, out-game-play, out-aggress people who set up the systems, made the rules, and have the power. Like with my previous client, I suggested she stop thinking there was a way to convince them she had what they wanted and shift her energy to the people and work that accepted her experience and knowledge.

To combat the tendency to doubt your inner wisdom, circle back to when you first got the message not to trust yourself. Usually it was an authority figure in your childhood, like a parent or guardian who passed on their own fears, or a teacher who judged you based on inaccurate stereotypes. If you can find the origin stories, you can interrupt their effect by recognizing you are now an adult and can choose to honor your intuition. Listening to yourself means understanding and tending to your feelings. Most people are "feeling illiterate" because society rewards thinking and attaches feelings to those who are seen as less than—children, women, and BIPOC. Even if your inner wisdom is screaming: *Listen to me!* you can easily rely too much on logic.

Your intuition is integral in identifying alternate solutions in difficult situations. It is like the light at the end of a tunnel, giving guidance to complete the action in front of you. It will also prompt you when you need to pause. This pattern of action and reflection allows you to take in small pieces of information with your heart, mind, and spirit so you aren't rushing forward with only what your mind tells you.

When I get caught in a busy, reactive mindset, my pause and reflect practice gets drowned by fear. As an entrepreneur, this can happen when my cash flow slows down. Institutional and cultural imperatives based on white supremacy reward production and speed, not thoughtful consideration, emotional intelligence, and collective support. An important shift for me to trust my inner wisdom was moving from saying "I don't know" to saying "I don't *like* what I know." While initially disheartening, it now puts me right where I need to be—making decisions based on my current reality with my inner wisdom.

> Filters are permeable and allow for clarity and compassion while alerting you to danger and false support.

As you learn to trust yourself, you learn the difference between filters and defenses. Filters are necessary in order to eliminate the distractions that cloud your purpose. Filters are permeable and allow for clarity and compassion while alerting you to danger and false support. Defenses are rigid and a normal reaction to historical and ongoing trauma. In blocking out what hurts you, they can also stop what heals you. Learning who and what to filter out and when to defend yourself fiercely is a crucial distinction you make by trusting your inner wisdom. One of my self-defense instructors interviewed many women who were physically attacked, and they all said they had known intuitively danger was near and had ignored their inner voice.

Think of this shift as similar to when you have a familiar route to a destination. Imagine that as you exit the highway off-ramp, you see another road that might take you there in a more direct way. You don't know for sure, so you decide to go your known route even though you have an intuition it takes longer. After three times, you decide to try the new route and see it does save time. Exploring any set patterns in an area of your life activates your internal GPS to try others, so pick one that is most accessible. You can then press the zoom-out button (pause and reflect) to look at the bigger picture to see if there is a more direct route to your full-hearted goals. In practicing this, you discover more direct, energizing paths to reach your goals based on both your intuition and your thinking.

Practicing this in recent years, I've found that I more easily switch to "What can I do?" when my first and second plans fail me. No necessity for *I should have known*. Just gratitude for every moment of clarity and commitment to well-being, which Buddhists call *bodhicitta*, defined as the complete wish to overcome our emotional delusions to free ourselves and others from suffering.

There is no such thing as self-doubt. It is societally constructed, colonized doubt internalized by BIPOC, women, and others who experience oppression. What is often called self-doubt is simply a situation or task we have never done before—it is new for us and requires a learning curve and appropriate support. That is completely different than doubt based on power dynamics. This doubt can be addictive, and like most addictions, it is supported by a culture that feeds a sense of scarcity. Think of the sky as a metaphor for abundance and this doubt as a cloud that covers the sun. You have been conditioned to forget the true breadth of your resilient internal and external resources.

By focusing of your inner wisdom, you can access what is needed even with this oppressive doubt clouding the full splendor of your truth. Your heart holds you even as you struggle to unchain your mind from years of relentless oppression. Identifying what situations and which people shake your confidence and developing a plan with those who love you is a crucial antidote. I coach my clients to prepare, adjust, and assess until it becomes a natural response when fear or dread show up. The goal is to notice sooner when you are disconnected from your inner wisdom, take time to rest, and then put your time and precious energy into your spheres of influence.

Ready for a #fullhearted breakthrough?

Doubt shows up when I...

My intuition has been telling me...

I can develop my inner wisdom by putting more time and energy into...

Do it.

Pick an amulet/object to carry with you that reminds you to trust your inner wisdom.

12

Accept Your Right to Flourish

> Be passionate and move forward with gusto every
> single hour of every single day until you reach your
> goal.
>
> —Ava DuVernay

*F*AKE...POSER...IMPOSTER...THESE WORDS MAY BE
lurking in the corners of your mind. This is the fear that you do
not deserve to be in the position you are in—be it at school or work
or any position of success and authority. If so, then you may have a
touch of the imposter syndrome.

You were taught or caught the idea that you were lacking an
essential element to being successful and you believed it. You then
created another image of yourself and fed it every time alleged proof
of your inadequacy showed up—basically when you made a mistake,
especially if it was pointed out by someone with institutional or
cultural or familial power.

You become a loner in carefully crafted ways by not showing
fear and believing others have no fear. You may have wonderful
achievements, both big and small, as mothers, as business owners,
and as community members, but you don't accept them because you

think you couldn't possibly be that successful. This is often based on your community's history of little access to resources and even less permission to have and express pride in your accomplishments. You credit people, events, luck, or God. You develop an aversion for that place where it's likely that you'll make mistakes and instead hang out where you are more likely to know the answers. Why? Imposters can't lose—it blows their cover.

Reality is, you have to lose! Money, relationships, work, ideas, love, and most of all, certainty. You begin to live with an explicit awareness that nothing is certain. This realization and constant practice have challenged me many times. I used to be a terrible loser because I did not get the message that losing could be a door to an important lesson about myself, others, and society. As a writer, I have been rejected endless times from residencies, agents, and publishers. This helped me get clear that I will be rejected and I will also stay on my path. I still don't enjoy a "no," *and* I know it is not a reflection of my talent or worth. It reflects the pervasive whiteness in the publishing industry, both in terms of the workforce composition and the books given access and resources.

One thing an imposter image is good at is accepting blame, shame, and guilt. For example, at a staff retreat, I ushered a Latina supervisor out of the room because her staff was going to surprise her with flowers and appreciations. As we left the room, she said, "What did I do wrong?" This is a favorite quote of the imposter syndrome.

As we waited for the signal to re-enter the room, she said: "I hope they aren't going to do something bad to me."

I chastised her: "Why don't you think of something positive instead of worrying? Besides, I wouldn't let that happen on my watch."

I paused, hearing my judgmental, patronizing stance, and switched the channel to compassion: "I have those thoughts too, it is an old script in my head. It never goes away, but I catch it sooner and sooner, and so will you." I understood she was used to expecting something bad to happen because she did not yet believe in her right to be a leader. She had not grown up seeing or having supervisors with her demographics.

There is a Buddhist precept not to praise self at the expense of others, but this does not mean not appreciating your effort and success. What it does means is you are not unduly boastful of your success *or* of your errors, which is—surprise—another way of praising yourself: *Look how good I am at being stupid or clumsy or inattentive.*

I did not truly believe in my intelligence until well into my thirties. My mother nitpicked at my sense of worth partly because of her sense of inadequacy as an immigrant with a thick accent and partly because she saw me succeeding in areas she could not. She would always want me to dress up more and was not pleased when I embraced my curly hair or chose to major in Creative Writing. A typical presumption is that you must do better than your parents, and that means earning more money and having a more impressive career. This can lead to competitive energy between children and their parents, as it did for me. I now think I did do better in that I chose a path that was not on the beaten path, but was instead guided by my purpose. My mother was an artist in her spare time, and I did better in that I embraced my creative life as essential.

I also internalized subtle messages from media and from my lived experience that Latinas were not meant to be much more than farmworkers, office help, childcare workers, or maids. Even though I attended first La Verne College and then Stanford University, my jobs included dorm maid, work-study office assistant, church service child care provider, and fast food cook. These were the jobs that people in privilege assigned me and I did not have any role models to inspire me to want or ask for more.

I had one professor during my undergraduate time in college who was a woman of color, and none when I received my MSW. By the time I entered my MFA program, I insisted on having my two advisors be women of color. By then, I knew that role models who had navigated the storms and deserts I was facing were key to my believing in myself as a writer.

Gabby Douglas, the first African American to win an Olympic all-around gold medal in gymnastics in 2012, said in an interview: "I loved Dominique Dawes. She inspired me to do bigger and better things." Dawes, the first African American to win an individual gymnastics medal at the 1996 Olympics, cried her way through an interview after Douglas' big win. "I think what touches my heart the most is knowing that there's a whole generation of young kids looking up to her as they looked up to me," she said. In an article on role models, Oprah named Maya Angelou as hers: "Over the years, she has taught me some of the most profound lessons of my life: that when we know better, we do better; that to love someone is to liberate, not possess, them; that negative words have the power to seep into the furniture and into our skin; that we should be grateful even for our trials."

Without role models to affirm your way of being, your inner critic will point you toward the direction of what you know and keep you playing small. Accepting your full worth means getting out and playing the game, whether on a sports field or in your evolving career. I still channel the Maude character in the cult movie *Harold and Maude*, seeing her push Harold to overcome his imposter syndrome. "Everyone has the right to make an ass out of themselves. You just can't let the world judge you too much." Later she tells him: "Reach out. Take a chance. Get hurt, even. But play as well as you can. Go, team, go! Give me an L. Give me an I. Give me a V. Give me an E. L-I-V-E. LIVE! Otherwise, you got nothing to talk about in the locker room." If you relinquish your well-crafted disguises, you *will* get hurt. The difference is that you are not as surprised because the imposter no longer convinces you that the messiness of life is bad and to be avoided. When I experience multiple disappointments in quick succession, an ache seeps down to ignite the small remaining embers of my imposter syndrome. *You see*, it says, *you were unlovable all along*.

Rather than sitting in the isolation of my imposter pit, I now know to engage in my antidote activities. For me that means meeting my sadness and rage with love and compassion rather than minimizing the impact of institutional and structural glass ceilings. I sift through the disappointments to see what I can learn. I often do 10-minute free writes to move me through the pain to a bigger vision that can sustain me.

Besides my personal antidotes, the core action is to go talk about it in whatever constitutes your "locker room" of people committed to full-hearted living. Being vulnerable can be scary because you have to trust your community will not judge you because of their own internalized insecurities. The roots of teasing or harassment from our families often comes from their own imposter syndromes. My clients often think they are bothering people by asking for support, rather accepting this as a reciprocal process. When I ask them if they think people are bothering them when they ask them for help, they often laugh and say: "Of course not!" We dig into the origin of this thinking until we get to their tender spot and then they instinctively know who to go to for support. Stay. Breathe. Trust. Maybe have a dance session or sing an uplifting song.

Challenging as it can feel, be grateful for every chance to play the game. Show up messy. There will be tears. There will be bruises. You can grieve and receive comfort rather than "suck it up." This is one of the biggest hurdles for my clients— "hanging in there" instead of letting go of the branch and exploring your actual reality with curiosity. How you honor the quiet, daily disappointments and moments of sadness strengthens or weakens your capacity to manage the bigger ones.

I had a client who had as one goal to take stock of her career and find a new job. She named her obstacle as being frozen by a pattern of "I can't do X because of Y." She would then not do Y and therefore never do X. Since she was a writer, we worked with free writes to unmask her imposter syndrome: *When did I decide other peoples' time is more valuable? What will be enough acknowledgement? When did I decide I had to prove myself? When did I decide I had to figure it all out by myself?* Because she did not respond to my worksheet questions to name her internal and external resources—as if she had none—we worked at cultivating kindness practices like sleeping enough and connecting with people who believed in her talent.

THAT ONE THING... I was busy giving in to Impostor Syndrome and not applying for the job I wanted. I remembered how many times Linda reminded me that I have resources; that I have so many good contacts. I had run into an old boss and we were talking about whether I was going to apply for the job. I told him that, rather than thinking about applying, I had been making a list of all the people I thought would be better at the job than I would, and he said it must be a very short list. That night, I thought about what he said and thought about Linda reminding me about the great contacts I have and how I should use them. I asked him and three other friends/former colleagues in the field what qualities I have that would make me a good fit for that position. They sent the most amazing, eye-opening, helpful responses! And, when I got called for the first interview, I reached out to the four of them again to send me questions they thought I should be prepared to answer. I have never felt so well-prepared for an interview in my life!

The work we did together continues to help me, especially now that I'm in this new job. This is the biggest job I've ever had, and just the idea of it can be super daunting for me sometimes. When I feel La Impostora creeping in, I think about the work I did to get this job and that makes me remember the work I did with Linda, and that always gives me ideas for how to dive back in and get past my doubt. Truly a gift that keeps on giving!

Imposter syndrome is tough to release completely, but it can be reduced to a breeze that comes and goes. Have tea with your discomfort rather than trying to ignore it or rush to a quick resolution. If you let go of the trap of urgency, spaciousness opens you up to search beyond your usual patterns for new possibilities. Give yourself multiple chances, especially since society may not do so because you don't fit the profile of what success looks like. Environments that do not value your demographics feed your glass ceilings and constrict your right to flourish. Your goal is to both stay with your truth and know you did your best to be heard. Make sure to make a pact with others to always support each other when raising a challenging issue.

Nevertheless, every setback offers information that can help prepare you for the next time you encounter a similar situation. Since you know better after each setback, you can be ready rather than surprised when people with power and privilege try to shut you down. Building your capacity to assess a situation with a structural lens rather than a personal one refutes the imposter's view of yourself as not having value.

When the syndrome shrinks, you can accurately assess when you have a steep learning curve and ask for what you need while also giving yourself a reasonable timeline to fully understand your work. Clients constantly get new positions and expect to figure everything out quickly for fear of being seen as an imposter or "unqualified" affirmative action hire. We discuss a realistic timeframe and supportive people so they can maintain an attitude of kindness as they learn and flourish.

You know the imposter is manageable when you shift to taking something well rather than hiding it well. You call the people who will support you rather than the ones who will feed your doubt. You accept that you lack nothing and acknowledge your brilliance even if no one else, loving yourself in each moment, regardless of the circumstances.

> You know the imposter is manageable when you shift to taking something well rather than hiding it well.

Ready for a #fullhearted breakthrough?

My imposter syndrome shows up when...
My healthy ways to manage disappointments are...
My role models inspire me to...

Do it.

Ask someone you trust to review something you created/wrote/are developing.

13
Appreciate Humor

Like a welcome summer rain, humor may suddenly
cleanse and cool the earth, the air and you.

—Langston Hughes

TO ENGAGE OTHERS WITH confidence, your relationship
with humor will allow you to maintain lightness with life's
disappointments. Do you know what your natural skills are in this area,
as opposed to what you experienced in your family or community? It is
much more than being able to tell a joke. Humor is an internal practice
that allows you to live without allowing the heaviness of oppression to
cloud your vision. For example, many friends and I often check in with
each other by sharing the latest subtle aggressions,
which I have called "paper cuts" for many years.
It helped me know the sting was not imagined.
I co-created a performance piece laced with
humor about some of our most irritating daily
aggressions. Not only did we laugh, we gave
space for our audience to both feel validated and
to relieve some of the pressure that builds up
from managing these moments alone. Humor is

> Humor is a
> solidarity tool
> to help your
> community lift
> the collective
> burden of
> oppression.

a solidarity tool to help your community lift the collective burden of oppression.

In days past, the court jester was to be both entertaining and realistic; all the other court functionaries cooked up the king's facts before delivery, but the jester delivered them raw. The jester was expected to say the plain, unrefined truth. And while sharing the raw truth is not always the best approach with others, a finely tuned internal jester is a requirement for breaking through your own glass ceiling. Unhampered by delusions, this jester will help give you the confidence to make decisions based on reality, no matter how difficult.

I'm pretty funny, and my mom was funny too. We shared a slapstick kind of humor that played off some of our societally instilled awkwardness with our bodies and identities. On a core level it stemmed from thinking we were supposed to make everyone feel okay. When I heard my mother talk about her childhood, she always interspersed the sting of the disappointments she'd endured with a story about, for example, how she released frogs in her boarding school to delay a test she hadn't studied for. I also remember the story of her putting white powder in baggies and slipping them into her office mates' drawers, joking that she'd brought them cocaine from her visit to Colombia. This tempered the judgments and stereotypes of her home country and gave her the power to create the joke rather than be the recipient. I also understood how her humor served to distract attention from the English she never mastered despite years of effort and gave her the courage to not stay quiet.

In my case, I was the class clown, distracting the boys from the fact that I was smarter than they were and providing a release for my sense of discomfort in knowing my family was not like those portrayed in the school books we used or the TV shows we watched. At parties when I was older, I was always one of the few BIPOC in attendance, and humor was a crutch that helped me manage that reality. Because the inequities in my life were unacknowledged, I pretended, along with everyone else, that my humor was not an attempt to please other people, especially those with more power and privilege. I acted as if we were the same despite clear evidence this was not so. At the time I thought that was the only way to survive and I relied too heavily on external validation.

Humor that emanates from an unconscious need to keep others amused can harden and become a mask that hides the resentments and fears that diminish your spirit. Making others laugh is a great way to feel that you have value, but it does not always help you heal. Maya Angelou spoke about a woman she would watch who looked like she was laughing, but upon closer observation was really crying. Humor can be sadness turned outward for protection.

How do you know you are using humor as a shield? The point of a mask, like a clown outfit, is to assume a persona with the purpose of making others have a reaction, in this case to laugh and be amused by you. Jokes that fall flat are mortifying because you have failed at your task and the mask may fall off and unwillingly expose your true self. Humor can be a core tool of the imposter syndrome, so when you can laugh off a "bad" joke, you know you are moving to a stronger relationship with humor and yourself.

In terms of humor that is mostly entertaining in nature, there are some points to making sure it is not detrimental. First and foremost, make sure *you* enjoy your humor. If others laugh or celebrate it, that's great, but not necessary. You may even be the only one laughing, and that is okay with you.

A method many use of entertaining others is to make fun of yourself. This is not always a good option. I spent years learning to be my own best friend and saying positive affirmations in the mirror: "I like myself, I like myself, I really do like myself." Now I'm going to put myself down on purpose? Maybe that works for Michael Phelps, swinging his five hundred medals on his finger and saying: "Oh, it was nothing." However, as a short, silver-fox Latina, I get deprecated all the time so this humor can reinforce stereotypes I am working to challenge. While many articles laud humor, they don't look at the power dynamics that can ignore the reality of inequities, like the following example:

Work vs. Prison

In prison, you spend most of your time in an 8 x 10 cell.
At work, you spend most of your time in a 6 x 8 cubicle.

In prison, the reward for good behavior is time off. At work,
the reward for good behavior is more work.

This kind of humor is not innocuous, it denies the reality of what being in a prison is really like and the mass incarceration of black and brown men. Humor is part of a larger social and political landscape and it requires our attention to ensure we don't minimize the anguish of inequities.

To use humor as a component of confidence, first take time to understand the role and history of humor in your life—more than anything, the legacy of how you relate to humor. My mother would joke about herself or her culture. The implied lack of self-value in these jokes mocked her, my dad, and her three children. As an adult, I understood she was protecting herself. As a child, I used humor to draw the attention of people in power away from my differences that might make them uncomfortable. While this protected my mother and me to some extent, it also left scars. For most of us, the humor that is most memorable is the humor that has hurt us, creating wounds that limit our relationship with our natural sense of humor and with others. Taking the time to reflect on these moments can open the path to appreciating humor in your life.

The first step I made toward changing my relationship to humor was not engaging when my parents invited me to mock the other one as if it was a contest and they needed me to break the deadlock. Fueled by my budding feminism in my early twenties, I stayed quiet or shifted the conversation when they used backhanded humor to hurt the other. I could most easily read my mom behind her mask and see her trying to defend her fierce spirit. Much later, while researching and writing my memoir, I also understood they had been wounded as children and by a country that did not value them as immigrants or ESL speakers.

Even as I have worked through my relationship with humor to ensure it is self-reflective and genuine, my adult children never hesitate to point out when it feels like it is at their expense. It is heartening, although not fun, that they share the impact regardless of my intent. They "give it to me raw," and I appreciate that they have the trust in me and the confidence in themselves to do this.

Humor can either soften or sharpen the truth, making it a challenging communication tool, and yet helpful when handled well. There is endless research that proves what we all know—humor and laughter is good for us. Full-hearted laughter opens our hearts, minds, and spirits, fueling all kinds of healing and transforming tragedy into joy. It is worth discovering the absurdities of life to give you a broad view of your life and to the vastness of joy to heal.

THAT ONE THING... I felt that having fun was indulgent when so many people were suffering. Linda helped me see that if I framed what made me laugh as a negative, I would not make space for joy. I slowly made time for humor and understood how it strengthened my capacity to stay healthy, happy, and whole. This then helped me balance my tendency of being too serious so I could sustain my work over the long haul.

Understood and consciously used, humor can be a wonderful tool. Natural humor allows our genuine self to emerge and take a long view of the absurdity of our delusions. Part of a full-hearted life is loving ourselves enough to not taking ourselves so seriously. Look around and identify who and what makes you laugh and the value it adds to your life, especially when you manage daily aggressions. Laughter is a great breathing practice, something we easily forget—that's why a "belly laugh" feels so good.

Ready for a #fullhearted breakthrough?
I use humor as a mask when...
Authentic humor allows me to...
I easily laugh with...

Do it.
Watch something or talk to someone today who makes you laugh.

Section 4

Consistent, Mutual Relationships

14

Enter and Leave with Grace

Entering and leaving are important aspects of any relationship and have to be given strict attention. Entering properly means being embraced, adequately oriented, and helped. Leaving properly means moving on without any outstanding issues, rancor, or feelings of unfinished business.

—Luis Rodriguez

W E SELDOM THINK ABOUT the way we enter and exit relationships—be they personal, professional, or in other realms—but this can have long-term consequences, especially in our personal relationships. There are significant factors that make them beneficial or not, especially because they are often tied to dynamics of power and decisions made by others.

I bet you can name multiple examples where there was little or no attention given to enter or leaving and the fallout still lives inside you. Further, you can probably think of how you were both a victim and a perpetrator of poor beginnings and harmful endings. Before discussing the damage and opportunities to heal, let's look at why it is important to give concerted attention to the way we enter and leave a situation or relationship.

Entering properly means being embraced. That is a powerfully intimate image. It brings up a sense of belonging, where you don't feel your most pressing obligation is to accommodate others at the expense of your truth. You also don't ask that of others—a challenging goal in a society still rife with power inequities. When you enter well, you have space to move to your own rhythm while seeking harmony with those around you. You aren't required to shrink your differences to assimilate into the dominant culture. To enter well means both being alert to a group or organization's capacity to support you and curious about how your talents can be integrated into what already exists. Not easy.

One client was wooed into leaving a good position by an opportunity to lead a racial equity program in a major arts organization. She came in and began to lay out a vision based on what the CEO had shared and her own deep experiences with art and racial justice; building relationship with her staff and reaching out to communities of color. As her influence expanded, her boss began to report that my client's colleagues did not feel she was a team player and to minimize her accomplishments. Soon enough my client knew she had been expected to assimilate. Since she didn't, she and her vision were not going to be embraced.

Having been in similar situations, I agree with the Spanish idiom that says: "Mejor sola que mal acompañada"—better to be alone than in poor company. In following the wisdom of this saying, I urged my client to keep seeking those who have a similar vision of equity, prosperity, and well-being for all to manifest her "body of life." This is advice I remind others and myself to practice.

For example, I have entered several relationships with tennis coaches. The first significant one was through the Berkeley Parks and Recreation Department. I had been playing with a friend and a man walked up to me and said: "I can fix your serve if you want."

In essence, he was inviting me to enter a relationship. Men typically offer me advice without asking if I want it, so his approach was already different and appealing. He was connecting to my unspoken wish to be better. He saw it in my body and my energy, as a good coach can. I signed up and took his classes twice a week for several years. He was both kind and unrelenting in pushing me to face my physical and emotional limitations again and again, always orienting me with specific help that changed as our relationship grew.

There came a time when I decided to leave his classes, as I had been invited by another student to join her team and compete in USTA matches. A good exit was possible with this coach because we had established an honest rapport from the beginning, and the ending moved me to the next stage of my growth, which he supported. His attitude contrasted with what can happen instead, when people discourage you from leaving based on their wish to keep you playing small or feeding their ego.

We tend to forget that most new beginnings include a leave-taking. How do we move on without outstanding issues, rancor, or feelings of unfinished business? Leaving is just as intimate as entering. Leave-taking with grace and power means departing resolutely out the front door, as opposed to sneaking out the back door. This means taking time to retrace your path slowly enough to acknowledge and resolve any outstanding issues. In addition, leaving with integrity means not focusing primarily on others' comfort instead of your own needs. Let people grapple honestly with the factors that may have caused you to leave. Your job is to leave, not to fix everything before you do.

I have worked with many clients who left their positions, including that of executive director. When you are leaving a place where you have been a leader, the tendency is to make a final mark, in order to demonstrate just how worthy you were to have that position. When you are not trying to prove your worth or get that last morsel of external praise, you can exit differently. You can focus on transferring your responsibilities and projects appropriately within the organization rather than thinking your work will continue as if you were there. Otherwise, you may stay longer than you wanted or be disappointed when you depart and your legacy is not affirmed.

When an exit is poorly managed, rancor is difficult to avoid and even more challenging to resolve. Rancor is defined as an angry feeling of hatred or dislike for someone who has treated you unfairly, and bitter ill will. These are important moments for reflection, yet they can also be clouded by your tendency to take too much responsibility and therefore let embarrassment or shame take over the narrative.

I certainly did not consider my career trajectory would ever include being suspended, demoted, and fired. I have always worked hard and focused on integrity and honesty. What I failed to factor in early in my career were the power dynamics that dictated whose honesty was allowed and whose was not.

In reflecting on my most unpleasant leave-takings, the pattern that emerged was that my experience of leaving was directly related to my process of entering. An example of an improper entering was when I did not support the hiring of an individual who was to be my supervisor. My current supervisor had worked under him and had seen numerous examples where he did not hold the confidentiality of clients in therapy. Because this was a small community, the consequences were often negative. When he started the job, word of me not supporting his hire was leaked to him and neither of us oriented nor helped each other. He insisted I fill out forms that were not required and when I pushed back, he told me he knew I had not supported him. My previous supervisor encouraged me to seek other employment and I was in that mode when he fired me for insubordination. I was full of rancor, especially because I had gone to the executive director the day before and he had encouraged me to keep fighting, but then did nothing when I was let go.

Over time, I released that rancor from my heart because bitterness only damages our spirits. Being treated unfairly is not an easy pill to swallow. Holding on to rancor is also a way to avoid the grief hiding behind it that also requires time and attention. It cannot be rushed. Leaving can be a salvation or a dirge, a joy or an experience that rips our heart to shreds. Buddhist nun Pema Chödrön states: "When things are shaky and nothing is working, we might realize that we are on the verge of something. We might realize that this is a very vulnerable and tender place, and that tenderness can go either way. We can shut down and feel resentful or we can touch in on that throbbing quality."

Conversely, you can stay in a situation that does not nourish you for fear you will not find a better work option, partner, or home, so much so that you don't even look. This scarcity mentality is one of the most important elements to release to break through your own glass ceiling. This can happen because you have the repeated experience of people in positional power undervalued you and you unconsciously believe you are lucky to be where you are, especially if they say that, as has happened with several my clients.

I had a client who was specifically hired for her expertise in the Latinx community. She spoke up at their diversity trainings and in her program meetings about how to shift the culture to better serve the organizations they funded. The feedback she received was that she lacked critical thinking skills and that she was so powerful that she shut people down.

THAT ONE THING... I was in an untenable situation with constant attacks on my character and minimizing of my accomplishments. Having done everything within my power to shift the situation, Linda encouraged me to seek other work and told me sometimes it is the right move to fold and leave. She reminded me there are no right words I could say when people were not interested in respecting me.

Truth is, you are entering and leaving all the time. Every time you enter or leave a room or office is a moment to apply attention. How you treat daily, ongoing entering and leave-taking can be excellent practice for the big ones that can either leave scars or inspire you to new heights. This means

> How you treat daily, ongoing entering and leave-taking can be excellent practice for the big ones that can either leave scars or inspire you to new heights.

creating intentional space between meetings and new connections to check in with yourself and assess your well-being. Do you greet people and check in with them before getting to the reason for the meeting or gathering? You can impact these interactions and your behavior does not have to be coerced by a results–oriented environment that minimizes relationships and building trust.

Death can be a daily part of your full–hearted life if you are open to seeing it. Apart from the deaths of thousands of beings in the world each day, there are the constant endings of work, relationships, and hopes in our lives and in those around us. Nature intertwines growth and death as natural and necessary. When I see dried leaves falling from trees as new buds are opening, I take comfort that I can manage endings better when I note they make room for new beginnings.

Regardless of how you have entered and left in the past, reflect now on the lessons you've learned and begin an ongoing practice. It is never too late to understand why past experiences still rankle you and how that rancor impacts your capacity to assess current situations. All that fuel burning in your heart from past harm can be directed toward igniting your passion. Like the small, natural fires that nature initiates to thin overgrown forests, processing and releasing old feelings can keep that rancor from igniting a massive conflagration. The new space that opens up after you burn through rancor is a better home for your life goals to flourish.

Most situations and relationships have a natural expiration date, but sometimes we don't leave due to loyalty to people or organizations. In these situations, your greater loyalty must be to your principles and values. If you are not allowed to do your best, then look for another option.

When you develop a practice of proper entering and leaving, your capacity to delude yourself about why you are staying or what you need to succeed in a new situation or relationship lessens. You stop falling into or staying in relationships with people or groups by happenstance or habit. This attention to entries and departures sets up relationships full of good will and mutual respect in your work and personal life.

I had a client who became aware that she had been conditioned as a woman to "suck it up and be a good team player" rather than embrace her voice and her leadership. We unpacked the insidiousness of the messaging that sexism could be overcome by doing what we are told will lead to success. She had applied to be an executive director twice and had not been chosen by mostly male board of directors. She saw how much her lingering rancor was influenced by her attempts growing up to gain her father's approval. I am always leery when organizations call themselves families. That may set up some dysfunctional authoritarian and loyalty patterns that are not helpful unless discussed thoroughly, something I have never seen done. Watch for how your family patterns influence your work dynamics and how change in one area will create opportunities for change in others.

No matter the circumstance, be it personal, work or extracurricular, you have the capacity to positively and thoughtfully influence entering and leaving with strict attention. You leave knowing you did your best. You enter asking for what you need to succeed. That is a gift worth giving and receiving.

Ready for a #fullhearted breakthrough?
I have unresolved rancor about…
What has expired in my life is…
I can enter a gathering with more intention by…

Do it.
Reach out to someone you really want to enter a relationship with or one you want to deepen.

15

Understand Your Friendship Paradigm

Each friend represents a world in us, a world possibly not born until they arrive, and it is only by this meeting that a new world is born.

—Anais Nin

MANY OF THE IMPORTANT relationships you have and will have, apart from your family, are your friendships. Because of the amazing potential of friendship, it is important to carefully consider this in all aspects of your life, including work. To understand your current framework, I suggest you go back to childhood. When I was a child, I believed in happily ever after with my friends unless one of us moving away, as some of my best friends did. With no Internet, and the vagaries associated with letter writing, these were not dramatic endings because they ended well. My unconscious framework remained until my mid-twenties.

That was when, during a phone call with a grammar school friend I had not spoken to in a while, I told her I was living in a house with my boyfriend and another couple. I felt her beaming on the other side of the phone. She had had several boyfriends and I had not—this one was, in fact, my first official boyfriend. Her response confirmed a suspicion I'd had, that she had judged me negatively over the years—she was pleased I was now part of the "attached to a man" clan. This showed me there had never been mutual affection between us. Now that I was doing what I was "supposed" to be doing, I saw the tangled strings attached to her conditional affection over the years. I cut them and her from my life, thus forming my first conscious definition of friendship—a friend does not approve of you only when you behave the way they behave.

In the coming years, my friendship paradigm became a conscious choice based on mutual, healthy self-disclosure. Beverley Fehr, a University of Winnipeg sociologist and author of *Friendship Processes*, asserts: "The transition from acquaintanceship to friendship is typically characterized by an increase in both the breadth and depth of self-disclosure."

Self-disclosure is a multifaceted word and has different meanings for everyone. What someone considers depth may be oversharing to someone else. No matter your definition, breadth and depth do require leaving familiar territory. bell hooks says: "The practice of love offers no place of safety. We risk loss, hurt, pain. We risk being acted upon by forces outside our control." For a long time I never told anyone about my internalized glass ceiling that had me feeling "less than." I never shared that I believed, despite evidence to the contrary, that if I just tried harder, I could avoid the slings and arrows of white supremacy. My practice of self-disclosure was terrifying and liberating as I slowly shared my fears in workshops and peer coaching provided by Visions, Inc., based in looking at how institutional and cultural privilege was responsible for many personal and interpersonal challenges. Having a safe environment was essential to cultivating healthy patterns of disclosure in my work and personal spheres. I slowly gathered a tribe that supported this intimacy.

The intimacy and honesty I had with myself led me to want it from others. I stopped having repetitive conversations based on past experiences or unmet needs. These conversations persisted because I cared for the person and hoped they could find their way out of the situation or relationship that they knew didn't serve them. I would push a bit to see if there was any interest in shifting and share some of my story of breaking out of my patterns, hoping our conversations would change. There was another kind of conversation cycle where I didn't share my full self because I had not gotten enough proof I would be seen and understood. Usually I had said something personal and they moved to a topic that was more comfortable for them. Unfortunately, more friendships than I wished reached a wall that could not be breached. I tapered off friendships and external commitments that did not match the breadth or depth I now required to reach my goals, which all included a racial equity approach.

There were people I began avoiding because they thought we had an authentic connection and we didn't. I hate being fake and I never wanted to bring up how wrong their view and experience of me was and how tainted by white supremacy they were. I especially couldn't pop the bubble that had them addicted to seeing themselves as a good person. There were also those who compared themselves to me or pushed me to be someone I wasn't rather than inspiring me to find my authentic voice.

Exploring my new inner worlds with the support of friends helped me center my friendship with myself and my values, breaking down the silos within myself that I had constructed to stay safe. I began living an openly spiritual life, bringing my curandera and my Buddhist teacher to my home for gatherings and ceremonías, inviting friends to events and sharing my journey in conversations and in my writing. I moved to where I wanted to live despite friends' disparaging remarks about the wealth and whiteness of Marin County, ignoring the natural beauty and small-town pace that led me there. Instead of paying for weekends away to write, my move supported me to deepen my writing life every day.

Loyalty in friendship is a double-edged sword. When I chose to study for my MFA, a good friend could not tolerate my limited availability for the duration of the program. It triggered a sense of abandonment for her that she had experienced in her childhood. I couldn't heal her wounds nor give up my dreams—neither is part of what friendship requires. Friendships will naturally ebb and flow as we change, and a mature friendship asks for and works with boundaries based on each other's current circumstances. Your friendship framework can create the sort of boundaries that allow you to be intentional in choosing friends and unconstrained by unrealistic needs on the part of others or outdated expectations.

Friendships in work environments have their own challenges. Dynamics of power are more likely to be in play, and loyalty can be difficult when disagreements can influence work security. I have had to rein in my tendency to share my vulnerability when my performance is being evaluated by someone who may not share my belief that this makes me stronger. Minda Harts, the founder of The Memo LLC, a career development company for women of color, states in her book *The Memo – What Women of Color Need To Know To Secure A Seat At The Table:* "When you're working in toxic environments, it's hard not to lean out. Deciding to stay or go is something that many of us battle each day."

In the very short *Mitta Sutta*, or discourse on friends, the Buddha tells his monks to seek out friends with seven qualities: "He gives what is hard to give. She does what is hard to do. They endure what is hard to endure. She reveals her secrets to you. He keeps your secrets. When misfortunes strike, they don't abandon you. When you're down and out, she doesn't look down on you. A friend endowed with these seven qualities is worth associating with."

This framework speaks to depth, breadth, and mutuality, three keys to healthy, vibrant friendships. It offers a foundation strong enough to withstand the inevitable gales of delusion about what friendship can be. For example, it can help you distinguish when someone protects you out of love and when they minimize your opinion because it threatens their beliefs. Courage among friends can undo the fear, embedded in most human psyches, that being right means we are worthy.

Taking time to decide what your friendship framework will be and to release or strengthen your friendships based on your current needs is essential to weathering the daily inequities of life. Notice if your friendships are all within a specific demographic of age, race, or gender identity and whether that supports your growth. Additionally, note friendships that only appreciate and make space for one of your identities and whether you may do this as well. Only engaging with a person's gender identity and ignoring race or class denies the intersectional, multidimensional people that we all are.

It is possible at times to find yourself in a "friend desert." This can happen when you have decided what you need and deserve and have stopped engaging with people who do not allow you to be your full self. You find yourself alone more because you are not allowing yourself to be distracted. You feel the hot loneliness. I remember being in a desert and sorting through my contacts, making excuses for others' failure to respond to my phone calls or emails. Continuing to give them the kindness and love I wanted made me avoid acknowledging our friendship had expired or turned into an acquaintanceship. It took practice to release my loneliness and transform it into an abiding, comforting solitude. I had to list and experience the benefits of being alone and the costs of unfulfilling connections. Less frequent intimate companionship with people who share your values and growth mindset is ultimately more soothing than shallow companionship. This is a good time to remember the bridge metaphor in the Be 100% chapter.

> Less frequent intimate companionship with people who share your values and growth mindset is ultimately more soothing than shallow companionship.

Margaret Wheatley, a writer and consultant who applies a lens of living systems theory to organizations and communities, states: "Despite current ads and slogans, the world doesn't change one person at a time. It changes when networks of relationships form among people who share a common cause and vision of what's possible. This is good news for those of us intent on creating a positive future. Rather than worry about critical mass, our work is to foster critical connections. We don't need to convince large numbers of people to change; instead, we need to connect with kindred spirits. Through these relationships, we will develop the new knowledge, practices, courage, and commitment that lead to broad-based change."

Two aspects of the friendships in all my communities is racial and cultural diversity and the commitment to physical, emotional, and spiritual well-being for everyone. This is what Martin Luther King Jr. called the "beloved community." It is essential when opening yourself to new world available through authentic friendships.

Ready for a #fullhearted breakthrough?
The people that make my mind and heart sparkle are…
The benefits of solitude are…
I will nurture my friendship with…

Do it.
Release your friendship with someone who only values the part of you that is like them.

16
Be Kind Rather Than Nice

Be kind to yourself, dear—to your innocent follies.
Forget any sound or touch you knew that did not help
you dance. You will come to see that all evolves us.

—Rumi

PEOPLE USE THE WORDS *nice* and *kind* interchangeably. Knowing the difference is fundamental to fostering your personal integrity and honest, meaningful interactions with others. Being nice or being kind are significantly different in intention. Nice emanates from the intention of pleasing others, being agreeable, and most importantly, being liked, as in the idiom to "make nice." There is nothing intrinsically wrong with wanting to please someone or be agreeable. However, when you do it from a place of wanting to being liked, it erodes your capacity to be powerfully present and grounded in your truth. Kind, on the other hand, emanates from the intention of being honest and having integrity, rather than of being liked.

My own path began with being raised, like most women, to be nice, coming from a place of wanting to be liked, of affirming my value externally. This meant being amiable in the face of subtle aggressions and keeping my mouth shut, as in: "If you can't say something nice, don't say anything at all." This saying appears in *Bambi*, when Thumper, who started out being appropriately curious and honest, was chastised into being nice.

Unlike Thumper, I didn't do well with this lesson. My need to speak my truth won out despite my strong desire to be liked. This resulted in ongoing problems with authority figures. I was dunked in my backyard pool by my mom, made to step out in the hallway by a teacher, and told to tone it down endless times at work and in my personal life. At work, I was propelled by values of justice and well-being for myself, the staff I supervised, and the resilient clients we served through programs and resources. I slowly came to understand over the years that some of how people reacted to my truth-telling at different jobs was tied to my lower power status. Privilege—granted by virtue of gender, race, age, and work status, to name a few factors—determines who must "play nice" and who gets to speak their mind.

If you believe you must be right and are given societal approval to behave that way, then integrity and being kind gets lost. Having experienced this model of leadership, one of my clients felt internal resistance each time she spoke her truth directly. She would then default to being nice rather than kind so as not to be seen as driven by power.

THAT ONE THING… I used to think that people were not going to like me if I was what I called "mean" or straightforward. Linda encouraged me to explore the origin of this childhood belief and to now use my privilege as a leader to practice saying what I thought directly. I found it was a relief to people when I was direct and didn't waffle due to wanting to be liked.

The effects of institutionalized racism had led her, like many BIPOC and women, to "play small" rather than claim her privilege and use it to foster a kind leadership model. By doing so, she modeled this for her staff and gave them permission to speak more directly and engage in discussions with open disagreement with respect along with an honest acknowledgement of hierarchy and decision-making options.

This shows up on many arenas, including how we respond to feedback on projects or passions that are dearest to us. After completing my MFA and sending my memoir to an editorial consultant, I wanted her to tell me how much she loved my book and to suggest agents, especially as I had worked on the manuscript for many years. While she applauded my writing, she homed in on how I could tell my story with a more intriguing structure and build my writing platform at the same time. I initially felt discouraged because I did not want to, basically, write another manuscript. Nevertheless, I took her words to heart and have since built a strong platform and rewrote my memoir several times to do justice to the story. If she'd told me what I wanted to hear, it wouldn't have helped me get to where I wanted to be in my career as a writer. My pride in my memoir, *The Cost of our Lives*, and my writing life overall germinated when Marcela Landres chose to be kind—she spoke the truth in a kind, rather than nice manner.

You may feel and be told you are ungenerous and selfish when you speak with integrity rather than from wanting to please. Setting boundaries is compassionate, but it doesn't always feel that way to those who encounter those boundaries, especially when you didn't use them before. The people who have been in your life longest will be the ones who will have the most difficulty in your shift from nice to kind. Be patient with yourself and them. Compassion requires courage, because when we are committed to genuine relationships, disagreements and trials are inevitable.

> Compassion requires courage, because when we are committed to genuine relationships, disagreements and trials are inevitable.

A Buddhist teacher gave me three questions to ask in order to decide whether to bring up a disagreement with someone: Is it true? Is it beneficial? Is it the right time and place? I use these questions all the time. When I decide the answer to all three is yes, then I speak, kindly, from my heart. Sometimes it takes me three seconds to answer those questions, sometimes three days.

Frankly, 80 percent of the time I answer the second question with a "no." That surprised me initially, as I used to think if something was true then it was always beneficial to share. I found there were three factors that helped me with question two: my experience with others' capacity to engage in honest conversations, the power dynamics between us, and my commitment to developing an emotionally intimate relationship with them.

To make these shifts, you must remember the high cost of being nice and relying too much on external acceptance. Not speaking your truths in order to please others can numb you to your emotions and place you in danger. While it avoids the necessary discomfort of disagreement, you also lose an essential aspect of truly authentic relationships. Doing so dims your brilliance and power and makes you less willing to be courageous in the future. Maya Angelou frames this wonderfully: "One isn't necessarily born with courage, but one is born with potential. Without courage, we cannot practice any other virtue with consistency. We can't be kind, true, merciful, generous, or honest."

How do you clarify whether you're in possession of the truth and when it's beneficial and timely to tell the truth? You learn by practicing, with as much courage, honesty, and wisdom as you can muster, to first tell *yourself* the truth. This means being kind, rather than nice, to yourself.

Then you can begin to do so when appropriate with others, including reflecting on what you learned for the next time rather than expecting perfection. This will likely carry risk since most people have not taken the time to make this an intentional practice. Pick situations and people that are low risk and let people know you are shifting. You take the pressure off yourself and reject the individualism of white supremacy by inviting others to be part of the change. The higher the stakes, the more important to make sure you have someone to practice with beforehand and to debrief with afterwards. Only take responsibility for what is yours when speaking with others, and do not do this work over email or text! This work is nuanced in ways flat communication channels cannot capture. It is also courageous work so be aware when you use text or email as a protection. When you are less kind than you intended or fall back into being nice, forgive yourself and make amends if necessary. There will always be opportunities to practice.

Not practicing can lead to continuing some damaging habits. For example, one unkind phrase I hear a lot is: "I lost it." What exactly did you lose? Your "niceness"? What probably happened is something occurred that violated your full-hearted truth and you responded in the best way possible given the external circumstances and your internal resources. This type of violation is usually a subtle aggression like being interrupted, talked over, or having your truth brushed off and then validated when someone else brought it up. It may have occurred five times that week and your "glossed over" nice collapsed from the weight of your suppressed rage, which is a consequence of not being true to yourself while debating how to manage power dynamics.

This unfortunately leaves you looking like you are "out of control" and so you say: "I lost it." Instead, slow down to retrace the trail of harm so you can understand what led to this moment. To develop and sustain a kindness practice requires definite intentions and evolving behaviors. Be honest when you reflect on your thoughts and actions each day. Acknowledge when you have made a misstep and take whatever action is required to get back in harmony with yourself first, and then with others who are committed to love and forgiveness.

Ready for a #fullhearted breakthrough?

I am avoiding conflict and calling it compassion by...
I numb my emotions with....
People who will be part of a needed change are...

Do it.

Set a time to meet with someone to discuss something
that requires attention and courage.

17

Support Your Whole Being

There is no thing as a single-issue struggle because we
do not live single-issue lives.

— Audre Lorde

THERE ARE MULTIPLE LEVELS to your whole being,
including your race, age, gender identity, education, class, and
country/cultures of origin—along with the family you were born
into and/or who raised you, the groups and communities you are
a part of, the neighborhood where you live, and the place(s) you
work. People in the many spheres of your life, including your service
providers, can nourish your purpose or poison your trust, making
caring relationships difficult to grow and maintain.

Supporting your whole being means first acknowledging all
the identities that matter to you and consciously noticing them
every day. Stephen Covey, author of *The 7 Habits of Highly Effective
People*, has a framework of roles and goals that I adapted because
my roles reflected a bigger, multifaceted life: mami of my two
children, family/community member, home goddess, entrepreneur,
spiritual seeker, athlete, yogi, writer, and happy, joyful being. That
extensive list didn't include other roles such as sports fan, Latina,

greying person, and bilingual, multicultural activist. Naming my multiple identities helped me see myself fully and notice which were either dimmed down by societal hierarchies or "overseen" by people making quick decisions about who I was.

In whatever way works for you, name, claim, and nurture your totality apart from what is praised or blamed by the external world. By embracing your complexity, you inspire others to do the same. You sadly will also uncover which identities people don't value. When someone I knew claimed herself as a biracial black woman, people responded by saying: "I thought you were Jewish" and "I thought you were Native American." Hidden in these comments was: "I don't want to see your blackness."

Refusing to be a single-issue person means understanding the duality and choice requirements of the dominant culture and how that harms you. This can be challenging, but it is worth the amazing possibilities you can develop for yourself and your communities. These norms insist, for example, that paid work is more important than parenting, and that following your passion, like I do as a writer, is foolish because it rarely results in monetary compensation. It ignores the multiple ways we receive compensation for living a purposeful life with multiple interests where, over a lifetime, you can explore many aspects of your "body of life." I remember reaching a point of desperation in my writer's life when I understood why some artists smoke and drink excessively, and yes, kill themselves. Most people don't pick the road less traveled for a reason. Supporting your whole being has a cost, but so does shutting off huge portions of your wholeness. Once you slowly accept your whole being, you also accept the complexity of others much better.

> Once you slowly accept your whole being, you also accept the complexity of others much better.

I had to slowly get to know different parts of my being and then, like a puzzle, align the pieces to make a whole picture. The value of recognizing and accepting our identities are two-fold. One is identifying where we have lost a crucial piece of our experience and wisdom, often tied to identities not valued in dominant culture, so we can reclaim it. I remember being asked in a workshop to remember my first experience of someone of a different race. I came up blank, and while painful, it helped me see how much I had taken on the white cultural norm of being color-blind to survive and delude myself that I was not the kind of different that was wrong. Unearthing this childhood wound led me to a journey of reflecting on my entire life to see what I had ignored to survive—being the daughter of Latinx immigrants, being bilingual, and being a female in a world full of gender violence.

Two truths that ruled me when I was younger and contributed to ignoring many of my identities was that white people would hurt me and white people would save me. I got these beliefs from my parents, who chose to live in a white suburb because they believed they would thrive better there. They worked with and for white people, but they never really trusted them. My parents watched their own backs and sent me the message that I should as well—while never saying this out loud. It took me a long time to develop truly authentic relationships with white people because they were as caricatured for me as I was for them. I could then begin the work of embracing my complex being without the need of a white savior.

Another value of recognizing and accepting our identities is that we can heal the wounds of compartmentalizing ourselves and feel the full power and joy of our strengths. As you explore your identities, you will find the lines between many are soluble—some identities remain static and some change. Class is a good example. You may have been born in one class and moved to another, like I did. Until I acknowledged the privilege of my graduate degrees and financial status, I carried the glass ceiling experiences of my previous status unconsciously. The impact was that I did not use my privilege for myself or for others. My healing has paved the way for my clients and many others to embark on their own journey of love and healing for future generations, as my purpose states.

To break through your own glass ceiling, unearth the negative messages about your identities so you can transform that toxic energy into supporting your whole being. Notice where you decided, based on external feedback, that you were not "enough" of a certain identity to claim it. Many of my mixed-race clients struggle to give attention to their multiple cultures and to fully believe in their right to claim their space. This requires eliminating a structurally imposed "either/or" paradigm, where survival means preferencing the identities that bring the most comfort to people in power.

As you explore your identities, remember it is not necessary to be all your identities all the time, just the ones that matter at that moment or with a particular group of people. This is not about hiding who you are out of fear, it is about making choices. My "life of the party" loud and silly persona waits quietly in a corner when I am in a silent Buddhist retreat sitting still for many hours throughout the day. When we learn to access our differences and similarities, then there is no normative mandate and we don't feed into stereotypes of ourselves and others.

One of my clients struggled to embrace her mix of identities, feeling she had less to offer than her co-director in an organization focused on ending violence against women and girls. I encouraged her to see how she may have internalized societal standards about her quieter, more analytical style of leadership not being as valuable. We also looked at the ways she was set up to compare herself with another woman of color as if there was not enough space for both to flourish. This resulted in her dimming her own light rather than seeing it as a wonderful compliment to her co-director's more exuberant style. It also meant she did not share her vulnerability out of a mistaken belief she was protecting her co-director.

THAT ONE THING... Being in a co-directorship can be hard in a culture that is constantly comparing you. My internalized inferiority would rear up, where I would often feel like my co-director was a better leader than I. Linda helped me see that as a habit of scarcity and that the work we do has room for all kinds of leaders. I stepped away from my ego and misgivings to embrace our collaboration. Linda helped me affirm my style of leadership and steered me away from comparisons to classic ideas of what and who a leader is. She helped me get clarity on my own vision of how I want to lead.

To assure I am embracing my full self and what I am capable of, I ask myself: Am I able to bring out my differences with this person or with that one, with this group or that one, with this work or that one, in this environment or that one? This practice continues because life is dynamic and my aspirations and needs change, along with my environment. One early practice to value my diminished identities was my decision in my mid–twenties to only read women and BIPOC, knowing I had been overfed on white privileged men. I have since expanded this practice to include social and cultural events, movies, clothes, food, and anything else I spend my time and money on to do my part to dismantle structural inequities. I work hard to make sure I am never the only one of anything and to preference places that make that easy.

Multicultural and multilingual lives require discipline to undo paradigms that force us into a monocultural "one size fits all" box. Identify where you have control and a plan on how to wisely choose the demographic mix across your life that honors all of who you are.

Ready for a #fullhearted breakthrough?
The people closest to me that minimize my full development are...
The dimensions of my whole being include...
The people who most nurture my whole being are...

Do it.
Do one action to embrace an identity that has been dimmed by societal values.

Section 5

Consistent, Persistent Action

18
Internalize the Secret of Discipline

> So let us plant dates, even though we who plant them
> will never eat them. We must live by the love of what
> we will never see. This is the secret of discipline.
>
> —Rubem Alvez

THE WORD DISCIPLINE OFTEN has negative connotations due to its connection to punishment. The definition I use is related to teaching, learning, and knowledge, along with mental self-control to direct or change behavior.

Even though both my parents were quite detail-oriented and disciplined, I did not understand the necessity of discipline to achieve my goals. *You can be so much better* was not a phrase I heard from teachers or my sports coaches. Without much encouragement to excel outside my home, I thought constant activity was the key to achievement. My parents didn't understand the American school system, but they did expect me to get high grades, often ignoring my "A"s and asking about the one or two "B"s.

Discipline is not a personality trait, it's a universal potential that shows up and must be nurtured differently in each person. In my case, engaging with it was initially an agonizing practice, as I feared it would stifle my creativity. When something interested me at school, I stuck with it until I reached a certain level of competence. Without being pushed by teachers or coaches to be the best I could be, I bounced around between different sports and activities. While I was competitive and liked doing well, I did not yet have the mindset to decide on a goal, assess the situation, devise a plan, and then evaluate the results. In hindsight, some of the low expectations I had for myself were based on my gender, class, and race. I had few role models, or even a visual of someone like me excelling. One of the reasons I loved the Olympics growing up is that it showed me a diversity of faces competing and winning. I now see that my parents could have been role models for me, but they were not held up as such in my U.S. education. They both started out at the bottom of the job market, my father as a dishwasher and my mother as a factory worker and house cleaner. While they had little formal education, they saved their money and bought a small house, eventually using the equity to purchase a fourplex. My father rose to waiter and then banquet captain at a fancy hotel. My mother ended up in a Kaiser Hospital business office as a clerk. She was such a hard worker they asked her to come back and fill in even after she retired. They lived by the love and example they planted in me and that I did not see or appreciate until I was much older. It took me years to understand all they had done to achieve what can never be taken for granted—a financially comfortable life in this country as immigrants from below the U.S. border.

There is a lot of talk about the lack of discipline in black and brown communities. Talk of how we are lazy, unmotivated, and don't believe in education. As I mentioned earlier, a key element to developing a strong discipline practice is having role models. An article honoring Lieutenant Uhuru from *Star Trek* as she turned eighty-two stated: "The Star Trek character played by Nichelle Nichols broke racial barriers on TV." When she thought of quitting the series at one point, none other than Martin Luther King, Jr., encouraged her to stay on. "He said I had the first non-stereotypical role, I had a role with honor, dignity, and intelligence. He said, 'You simply cannot abdicate, this is an important role. This is why we are marching. We never thought we'd see this on TV.'"

Many BIPOC, and blacks in particular, hear while growing up that we have to work twice as hard to get half as much. While that is an unfortunate reality in many situations, managing this pressure often results in over-efforting that hurts your health and relationships. This idiom is often exacerbated by the divisive stereotyping of the back-handed compliment of being called "the good one" or told you are "not like the others" of your race. This segregation often results in being separated from your tribe and then discarded as the "chosen one" when you are no longer needed. Resisting this throws you into the "chip on your shoulder", "overly sensitive", and "race card" categories. This is where discipline is not only about self-love, it is about surviving structural inequities.

The first time I developed a strong, conscious discipline practice was as a mother at the age of thirty-eight. Before that, I was impelled more by the end than by the means. Discipline is all about the means. In fact, when my partner and I knew we were having twins, I created lists, the first conscious discipline tool I used (other than a watch, timers, and alarms). If I hadn't made and then checked off my detailed packing lists for trips, they would have ended in tears and sad memories. Mothering also meant lots of mental self-awareness and control so that we created schedules that centered their needs—leaving parties so they had a regular bedtime, planning travel so they could nap in the car, and always packing snacks, drinks, books, and toys when we left the house. Repetition and boredom are necessary elements in achieving life goals and in raising children. Discipline habits force me to transform my world, one small change at a time; to plant dates, as the Rubem Alves quote states, that may not flourish for years.

I had a client who believed she had to make sure everybody else was okay, which meant she did not speak her truth often, offered help that was not requested, and then felt resentful. She was thinking of leaving her job and when no one wanted her position, she used this as a reason not to move toward the next step in her life. We explored how her mindset was detrimental to discipline, which is inherently based in self-love, not unnecessary sacrifice. She would take small steps to meet her personal goals, like taking one day to be with her friend, and then judge her actions by saying "it wasn't much." By denying the value of micro-changes in reaching her big goals, she constantly rained on her own parade. She kept at her discipline habits and eventually understood that her patience and fortitude allowed her to give more authentically to others. This shift in mindset meant she led by example more and less by molding her decisions based on what other people wanted.

Discipline requires imagining a different timeframe. It is a useful process for recovering "struggle addicts" like my client, who began celebrating each positive change and not obsessing about the next potential problem. It is essential to consistently claim what you do know and can imagine clearly. Then ask: "What am I willing to do to develop my gifts over time?" Discipline means getting to know what your excuses are so you can develop clear reasons why you are willing to release entrenched thinking patterns. What are obligations and/or promises you typically do not keep, despite your best intentions? What do you do instead of doing what you say you want to? This discipline self-reflection is best done with a curious mind and without blame or shame.

A typical excuse is seeing discipline as something only extraordinary people engage in. My intuition is that you already demonstrate discipline every day. To make it an explicit practice, I suggest you start with the first and last hour of your day. These are the most important two hours in creating a fruitful discipline practice and life. Make a list of what you are currently doing in these two hours. Rather than judging yourself, look at each activity and ask yourself: When did I start doing this and why? Do these activities bring ease, or do they encourage scattered energy? You likely have an unconscious routine that you can now observe so you can make conscious choices and commitments.

List and commit to activities that are essential to your well-being and note down optional, good choices. Order them in a natural progression. Some of my first-hour activities are to make my bed, light incense, and dedicate any good that I will do that day to someone to affirm my connection to everyone. One of my last-hour activities is turning off the text-notice sound on my phone and setting alarms for my next day's commitments. If your time is limited, I suggest you have several non-negotiable habits that stabilize your internal anchor. While every part of your day should be guided by your important values and goals, the first and last hours form the cornerstone of discipline. They enhance or confuse every other second of the day.

A typical barrier to a discipline practice is the notion that, with enough effort, you can reach a point where you achieve goals without effort. This does not mean that goals cannot be achieved with ease. Effort and ease are very different, and both are essential elements of a thriving discipline practice. Ease emanates from a mind and a spirit that rests like a giant tree amid the natural chaos of change. Effort is the energy that fuels creativity, planning, and right action. Create flexible structures that compel you to do what is good for you, bring the most ease, and use the appropriate amount of effort.

Treat your discipline habits as precious gifts. Discipline allows us to shift from having a busy, overscheduled life to creating a full, flexible life grounded in our purpose. Practice does not make perfect, what it does is sustains courage, joy, and inner confidence. Notice how your day, week, and life blossom with the secret of discipline. It often means living by the love of what we will never see—knowing our lives benefit by what was planted by those who came before us and knowing others will benefit from what we plant with discipline.

Ready for a #fullhearted breakthrough?
A negative message about my relationship to discipline that I can change is...
Some disciplined habits I already have are...
I can apply more discipline to...

Do it.
Ask someone in your life to mentor you with helpful discipline habits.

19
Know That a Yes Includes a No

> Shout out to everyone transcending a mindset, mentality, desire, belief, emotion, habit, behavior, or vibration that no longer serves them.
>
> — Lalah Delia

WE HAVE ALL HEARD someone (and maybe even yourself) say: "I have a hard time saying no." Conversely, we can say or hear: "I always say yes to new opportunities." One of the most profound lessons I have learned and practice every day is that *yes* and *no* are flip sides of the same coin. Each time you say "yes," you are saying "no" to something else and vice versa. To live a more purpose-driven life, you must take time to unearth the "no" behind every "yes" and the "yes" behind every "no." This is even more essential for people who have moved to a higher educational and/or class level than their parents and family. Many "one size fits all" self-help books and speakers do not delve into the impact of people who inherit the sense of feeling responsible for more than just themselves because of ongoing inequities. The pressure to uplift other family members or cultural communities is not as easy to say no to as these people would have you believe.

I constantly make tough decisions related to my social justice commitments to say "yes" to a project that others would term optional, like my writing. Do I attend a rally for civil rights, or do I finish edits on my current book, which supports those who have been denied access to their civil rights? Do I write a letter to my ICE detention center pen pal or develop online courses to generate income from my books? When I pick the second choice, I remind myself that writing and promoting stories that are not heard enough in our society *is* an act of justice and joy. I also acknowledge that neither of my choices reaps economic benefits, which is my priority in a society that diminishes my worth and sets up structural barriers to my wealth accumulation.

When I decided to build my coaching practice, I moved my nutrition and well-being network-marketing business to the back burner, even though I dearly love my company and products. The clarity to do this came from a coach who pointed out that I was not fully embracing a gift that was right in front of me: my skill and dedication as a coach. This long-term side hustle was worth a great big "yes," so I created a specific plan to turn the heat up. This meant clarifying my new priorities to all my networks and developing relationships that would support my shift.

To keep your ambitions realistic, you must make decisions that allocate your resources and time well and keeps economics as a priority. The hardest part may be saying "no" to groups who have been a support for you or bring you joy. If so, it helps to know you are not saying "no" forever, you are building success in another area of your purposeful "body of life." Remember that every decision is written "in pencil" and can be re-considered.

It helps me to imagine my life as if I am preparing a multiple-course meal all day long. Family plans and work deadlines are constantly baking at low heat in the oven while pots on the stove are full of current writing projects, exercise, home chores, and friends/community. I also have writing projects and income generation opportunities marinating in the refrigerator alongside raw ingredients for possible collaborations and surprise dishes.

To reallocate your time and passion realistically, commit to tools and accountability partners that support you to weigh the pros and cons of each "yes." If you don't, the hidden "no" behind every "yes" will lead you to burnout, resentment, and disappointment. The stove is a perfect metaphor for what happens when I don't pay attention to both sides of my coin—burnt tortillas, unevenly baked self-care, and lots of singed relationships.

The good news is that the practice of looking for the flipside of every "yes" and "no" will help break through unhealthy patterns, creating a more thoughtful explicit relationship with decision-making. I remind my clients time and time again when they struggle to practice self-care that this inward focus also supports their life work. One of my favorite hashtag is #selfcareiscommunitycare.

Let me unpack two entrenched patterns from my coaching practice. The first one is demonstrated by one of my clients who sees and personally experiences a world full of inequities due to her immigration status. She had been accepted into a residency program for activists to take time away to truly rest. I coached her when she returned to solidify her renewed commitment to self-care in her everyday life. What she learned was that the flip side of a zealous "yes" to social justice inadvertently became a "no" to self-care, which kept joy at bay by pushing her to ignore her needs. Lena Horne, a singer, actress, and civil rights activist said: "It's not the load that breaks you down, it's the way you carry it." By saying "yes" to fighting for others' civil rights, my client had unconsciously decided she had to say "no" to exercising those rights in her own life. When she understood this, she used this new paradigm to say "no" to overwork and "yes" to exercise and home-cooked meals. This rebalancing gave her the energy and joy to do her social justice work without resentment. Her frequent illnesses diminished, which meant she accomplished her work without the pattern of exhausting herself until she had to rest. She was more productive in her work because she was healthy and energized.

A second reason people carry the load heavily is their sense of "making up for lost time," a phrase that covers up unnecessary regret.

At one time I thought I had wasted my thirties. Why? I hadn't yet embraced my passion as a writer, mostly because writing was not valued as a profession in my family and community circles. I had played *too much* league soccer and tournaments that meant weekends trips away. Finally, I did not yet understand the importance of managing my money to create time and financial freedom rather than earning what covered my yearly expenses. When I reflected on this regret, I saw that my thirties work life was rife with poorly trained supervisors who did not support my talents and leadership as a woman of color and therefore I did not develop authentic confidence. I still believed in the level playing field as preached by my immigrant father. He saw me as not having the struggles he had and encouraged me to tell the truth without considering power inequities that trumped my educational and English proficiency privileges. He supported me to be an athlete and embrace my physical being and the lessons sports taught me about mental focus and learning to lose and win well. In addition, my assertiveness was rewarded on the soccer field as I was not at work. I understand now how sports serve as a culturally accepted outlet for rage, both in healthy and in violent, abusive ways. Because I experienced negative consequences at work for speaking out, my finances suffered. I moved past the regret by assessing my conscious and unconscious "yes" and "no" decisions of that decade with compassion and shifted to living out my lessons learned.

One of the keys to understanding the relationship between "yes" and "no" is recognizing the past and current context of your life and where there is urgency with timeframes and your priorities. While there is time to manifest your "body of life" over the span of a lifetime, not all windows remain open forever. The danger of shouldering the "super person" paradigm is that there is a limit to how much mental and psychic

> The danger of shouldering the "super person" paradigm is that there is a limit to how much mental and psychic energy you can expend, even if you love and choose everything in your life.

energy you can expend, even if you love and choose everything in your life. No matter how much external privilege and support you have, you are the one who must manage your internal journey. Assess your priorities and calculate the amount of energy and time your goals truly require to be achieved.

One of my clients had a long list of goals she wanted to complete, all of which pushed her out of her comfort zone and placed her in situations where she did not have role models who reflected her as a woman of color or who did not share her values. She remained steady in each "yes" despite multiple setbacks.

> *THAT ONE THING… Linda reminded me after each setback that a "No" can mean "Not yet." This awareness helped me deal with all the rejections and lack of responsiveness from faculty while writing my thesis and when fundraising for my first school board campaign and kept me going toward my "Yes" long-term goals, which I eventually achieved.*

Not surprisingly, saying no to what you enjoy and brings you benefits can be more challenging than saying no to what clearly does not serve you, especially if it has a touch of enjoyment. One friend acknowledged how she can "crowd out" new ideas with too much of what she has already created and where she experiences competence. When I decided to make more space for my writing, I released work that I did well but did not nurture me as it had in the past. I also said no to interesting options presented to me. It helped me immensely to create a simple script for opportunities that enticed me: "Thank you for thinking of me for [fill in]. I am committed to completing [fill in] this year. When my time opens up, I may consider this opportunity." Write all the yes/no scripts you need and see how entrenched patterns shrink and your commitment to your full-hearted goals stays clear. Remember you will likely encounter your own fear about saying yes to what serves you. Slow down and reflect when that happens, call someone you trust, be curious and open-hearted.

This allows you to share your lessons learned in reaching your yes and frees you from using regret as a no. By embracing each yes and its complementary no with intention and compassion, you live a life that transcends entrenched patterns and does justice to you and to others.

Ready for a #fullhearted breakthrough?

Habits that no longer serve me that I will practice saying *no* to are...

Places, people, and situations that push me to say *yes* when a *no* is more appropriate are...

A *yes* that can bring me joy is ...

Something I enjoy that I will say *no* to so I can focus on my top priorities is...

Do it...

Get an Accountability partner, re-consider changing the one you have now if they are not supporting your full being, or thank the one you have now.

20

Integrate Transition Time

> We must use time wisely and forever realize that the
> time is always ripe to do right.
>
> —Nelson Mandela

MANY PEOPLE HAVE HEARD the phrase to "read between the lines." A basic definition is understanding what is meant by something that is not said or written explicitly. While this has different meanings depending on the situation, I apply it to the invisible lines that exist between the tasks, appointments, and events in our calendars. To read between those lines, you must understand what dominant cultural norms stop you from doing this, especially the "being busy is the same as being productive," urgency-based model.

The most common impact that arises when you don't integrate transition time is negative stress, as in what happened to one of my clients. I first explicitly named the importance of transition time when coaching a woman working full-time and attempting to nurture her creative writing life. She expressed her frustration at her pace of production. I asked to see her calendar. She had nothing written during the daytime hours of the weekdays and had times blocked out in the evenings and weekends to write.

"Where," I asked, "are your work hours?"

She laughed, and then blocked out her work hours: 9:00–5:00. She had herself writing from 6:00 to 9:00 PM several days a week and could never start at 6:00.

"How long does it take to get home from work? To eat dinner?" I kept asking her questions until she saw how unrealistic it was to expect herself to begin writing sooner than 6:45 and that she needed to end by 8:30. Her previous plan hadn't included transition time for her to get home and eat, and then later on in the evening to prepare for bed, talk to her husband, think through lunch for the next day, and check her email. Who writes down transition time in their calendars? These conversations helped both of us to understand the value of being explicit about transition time and marking it in our schedules.

I used to blissfully start my day with the delusion that what was written down in my calendar would come to pass, but then bumped up against an invisible force field: something that kept my plans from unfolding as I thought they should. That something was often an accounting of my transition time. I now do my best to not schedule anything back to back, which naturally allows me to tend to my transition activities. Some of my transition times are between leaving home and driving out of my parking spot, between arriving home and sitting down to eat, between ending one phone call or video meeting and beginning another.

What have you not scheduled in today? Some possible activities are getting water and eating meals, going to the bathroom, processing feelings after a meeting you know will be challenging, and spending time in transit. How about finding parking or exiting public transportation and arriving at your destination? Allowing for transition time makes the full route of our days apparent, eliminates the nagging sense of being rushed, and gives time for our well-being habits.

Transition time is a large and significant part of each of our days—it could even be half of our waking hours. It is like the oil that greases the wheel—when we fail to include it in our planning, we stop and start through impossible agendas. We then personalize the problem, thinking that we are not organized enough, or worse, that life is too complicated to enjoy and we had better lower our expectations. We buy into the norms of overdoing and perfectionism, and then use guilty pleasures to assuage our tired body, mind, and spirit.

> Transition time is a large and significant part of each of our days—it could even be half of our waking hours.

A writing client would constantly delude herself into thinking, despite evidence to the contrary, that she could meet her creative goals regardless of her other time-consuming obligations. Driven by a sense of urgency, this pattern was endemic to her life and did not allow for a sense of accomplishment or an acknowledgement of how much she did with so few resources.

THAT ONE THING…I would constantly set goals based on unrealistic expectations of myself and an internalized pressure that I had to squeeze something out of every minute to feel productive. Linda encouraged me to set my goals differently—instead of saying I would finish editing my entire essay, I would commit to working on it for two hours or three times a week. "You can exceed your goals" was the sentiment that shifted my relationship with my accomplishments. Instead of feeling bad because I had not written every day or finished my editing (my previous goals), I rejoiced when I worked on it for three instead of two hours or wrote four instead of three times!

To read between your lines, release energy-draining, self-blaming thoughts and make room for a new way of working with time. There are some clear guidelines for reading between the lines that create a greater sense of ease as you move through each day's inevitably surprising journey.

Review each day before it starts, either at night or first thing in the morning. Visualize yourself going from each line item to the next. How long will it really take to get ready to start your meeting or tasks? Where might there be glitches? Set alarms to remind you of your calls or when to leave the house that consider all your transition activities, like getting your water bottle and putting on your shoes.

Schedule time between each appointment and meeting. No 9:00–10:00 and 10:00–11:00 drama. Go *wild* and break out of the on the hour and half hour scheduling: try out 10:10, 2:15 or even 5:20! Think about what you might need or want to do in between each line, especially those lines that you know will be challenging. Prep at the beginning of each day for all your meetings before the *first* one starts.

Transitions are opportunities to recharge, not distractions from our "important" goals. Keep empty space in your calendar or even put *TT*. This allows for surprises, which come as surely as heavier traffic on Friday afternoons. You can then be on time rather than continuously discouraged by being ten minutes late. You cannot know everything and miscalculations will happen—breathe before entering a meeting that has already started. Your energy is palpable and what is important is that you have arrived. Calmly take your place, leave the closest open space for whoever may arrive after you, and engage in the meeting rather than chastising yourself.

Another important shift is to eliminate the phrase "I don't have time" or "I'm so busy." That is a scarcity mentality. Own your relationship with your priorities and choices and your "no". Instead say: "I am not making time for" or "I have not yet made time for." Being clear-eyed about transition time will feed your soul and keep you from dissipating your energy with excess effort, apologizing, and self-deprecation.

This also means understanding your time shift aspirations based on your positional power and capacity to be fully in charge of your time management. Many of my clients work in cultures where meetings are scheduled back to back to back. You will have to assess your capacity, with the support of others, to raise conversations about the organizational culture and how meeting scheduling and attendance can be more effective. Work with what is in your hands to shift, like making sure you have planned your meals and brought your water. When I plan day-long events, I have organizational clients who ask me to make the lunch times shorter or to make it a working lunch. I explain the value of time off from the work to process, reflect, and build relationships. I will not budge from that, along with putting in breaks and playful activities to make sure people engage their body, mind, and spirit. When I attend a packed conference schedule, I go through the agenda and plan when I will give myself time to integrate, debrief with someone, or get outside.

Welcome transition time into your life with intention by beginning today to notice what is in between your lines, remembering that time between planned activities are moments that can either ground you or discombobulate you. Slowing down to observe life's transitions will ease that anxious itch and make you use your time wisely.

Ready for a #fullhearted breakthrough?

My biggest delusion about time is…

My usual transition activities are…

I can make my day a true reflection of what really happens by…

Do it.

Look at your calendar and see where you can build in transition time.

21

Aspire to Be Your Brand of Happy

> You are your best thing.
> —Toni Morrison

BEING TRULY HAPPY MEANS living out your own definition of joy and contentment. Therefore, it is grounded in being your true self, not in doing what others say will make you happy. Because our happiness is not in the hands of another person—or dependent on a specific outcome—it is a constant practice of self-awareness and patience. The more inequities you must manage, the more patience happiness might require, so an authentic, mutually loving community is essential to this aspiration.

Happiness was not something I thought about in an intentional way except as a child. I did want to be happy, but most people around me did not consider it essential to living like food, water, and rest. I received the message from my parents that hard work and thriftiness were essential to life, which the Catholic religion of my youth supported, along with penance for a multitude of sins. One of my parents' worst moments was when I left a county job with benefits and alleged job security, as that for them that would guarantee their brand of happiness.

I still sought happiness as a young adult, but it felt uncomfortable and decadent, especially as I continued working for justice in a variety of organizations and community groups. Joy seemed arbitrary, decided by someone else or tied to an external event, not a flush of peace that filled my soul and settled into me with gratitude. Discontent became a reliable state, one that was fostered by others who doubted the possibility of true happiness, especially when struggling with daily inequities. Nothing good felt sustainable; I was always waiting for the other shoe to drop.

By engaging in the practices in previous chapters, I understood happiness is an internal state, not a thing received from or given to others. The outcomes are quiet and usually only discernible by me most days. It can be raining negativity and you can be dry under an umbrella of inner joy once you have cultivated it. Happiness is a gift of being, not doing. The doing can be one of the means to happiness, but activity is too often mistaken for actual happiness. One of the important attributes to happiness is tending to mutually loving, beneficial relationships with people and nature, starting with yourself.

We often feel we are in difficult situations that make happiness impossible or selfish. I had to challenge all the fairy tales I was fed about what would make me happy and listen instead to my heart and to the teachers and guides who did not promise rainbows—they gave me stark truth and disciplines like meditation and spiritual rituals to see the fallacy of an easy road to happiness. Become aware of when you are struggling because of inheriting other people's definitions of happiness rather than doing the work of unearthing yours. While the past doesn't determine today or tomorrow, it does influence it. Take time to identify and address red flags in your work, family, and extracurricular activities and assess what is possible to shift toward a genuine capacity for joy. Go slow initially to decide what pace is needed to find the happiness in each moment.

It takes work to gain this joyful mindset. You must believe there is enough for you and everyone else to you avoid competing and comparing. Sometimes I must sit still as the itch of an old habit tries to woo me away from a path of joy. This means refusing to be sucked into conversations where the point is to malign others to feel superior. I still ask myself: Am I willing to sit with the tediousness required to nurture authentic happiness amid the sorrows of the world?

One of the biggest glass ceiling for my clients to break through is the one they internalized about joy. We all receive constant messages that there is a limit to how happy we can be in a world that is full of suffering, in workplaces where

> *One of the biggest glass ceiling for my clients to break through is the one they internalized about joy.*

emotions are measured out carefully, in relationships where we have been told we are responsible for keeping others happy at our own expense. Being happy appears easy but can be the toughest ceiling to crack. But crack it you must, as Yoda would say.

One client had many goals to accomplish and drove herself from one to the other without ever stopping to appreciate all she had achieved under difficult situations with little support.

> *THAT ONE THING…I appreciate the way you helped me recognize and celebrate my progress, even if it doesn't always look the way I thought it would. It helps me to remember to focus on progress, not perfection.*

Another client shared how she found happiness during a mini-flood she discovered one morning when arriving at work. After requesting help, her first impulse was to start cleaning up the water, even though she couldn't do much on her own. She decided instead to eat her bagel while it was warm. I love this story for all it teaches us about not letting what we cannot control have us miss our "warm bagel." I remembered this story when I was walking around my block the next week filled with anger at a racist encounter. Slowing down is so important when my heart and mind are racing, so taking walks is an essential part of my happiness practice. As my body moved, I was able to acknowledge and move through my feelings. I stopped to smell some roses and smiled, seeing how that idiom is not trite when your light is dimmed daily because of your hair texture or your skin tone. Happiness means smelling the roses, eating the warm bagel, and returning again and again to gratitude every morning that you are alive to the pain and to the beauty that exists in a full-hearted life. Enjoying the warm bagel is about making sure we feed our body, mind, and spirit in times of crisis. If not, then we do not have access to the skillful means required to make good decisions and find the joy.

I had a client who had applied as an internal candidate to be the CEO of an organization and was not chosen. The new CEO came in and was supportive of what my client wanted to focus on so the urgency to keep looking for another job diminished. We discussed the temptation she felt to settle for "low happy" at this job when "high happy" might be possible in another position. She appreciates the current situation while continuing to look for work that gives her more joy.

In living out these practices of happiness, you likely do not have sufficient boundaries to spend time cultivating joy. You may then shift to having too many boundaries as your inner happiness unfolds and you want to protect it from external forces. Finally, spongey boundaries appear because you know how to protect yourself with appropriate filters and access that quiet contentedness even in the toughest of times. You avoid isolation and separateness and can observe and participate in life instead of trying to control people, places, or things. You are ready to find the breakthrough in every day and share your joy so others on the path with you know they are not alone.

None of your ceilings are bullet-proof. They feel like it, but as you work with the practices in this book they can be as fine as spun sugar—consistent tapping may suffice. You don't have to work so hard doing what will give you no true relief. If you have gotten anything out of these words of mine, remember the power of tap, tap, tap. Each glass ceiling that cracks will send spiderweb cracks to others, and theirs to you. Just remember that demanding perfection of yourself and others is the strongest enemy of joy.

Every previous chapter is a puzzle piece of what nurtures happiness. Each moment of love and compassion you grant to yourself flows into the next until it is no longer a constant conscious effort, it is a life of loving your authentic self. Your brand of happiness is strengthened by the discipline of daily commitments. It requires a mindset of prosperity to live a full-hearted life as you claim and use whatever privilege you possess to further equity. While greed, hatred, and delusion will constantly distract your heart, by the same token generosity, love, and truth keeps you strong. Scarcity behaviors will naturally ebb because you give them less and less attention while building your power and voice. The question that underlies authentic happiness is: Where can I do the most good and experience the most joy for myself and others? You are always part of the equation.

Make no mistake, claiming your full-hearted self is not a quick fix. What keeps me going and I hope will keep you going is knowing as I break through my glass ceiling with happiness, I inspire others to do the same. You find your cracks are interconnected across minds, hearts and spirits; your efforts free others and their efforts free you to be your best self.

Ready for a #fullhearted breakthrough?
One unhappiness habit I am ready to crack is…
Some places in my life I am settling for "low happy" are…
My definition of happiness includes…

Do it.
Make and post a list of your Joy-inducing activities and leave space to add more!

133

Acknowledgements/Homenaje

To all my ancestors who broke through their own ceiling to give my efforts ease. To all children, who give me courage to break through my glass ceiling so their lives and those of future generations can be full of safety and love.

To my clients and friends whose bravery inspires me daily and whose breakthroughs join mine to shine brighter.

To the writers who take difficulties and trauma and make sense of it all with me and for all of us.

To all the people who say "that one thing" in the course of every day that soothes or inspires me. To my querida accountability partner and amiga Clara Angelina Diaz, who kept me on track and published an earlier version of a chapter in her book.

To those who read parts or all of this manuscript and gave me valuable feedback: Susan DeFreitas, Maria Ramos-Chertok, and Paula Farmer.

To Daisy Hernández, who asked me years ago: "When are you going to write that book?"

To all the people I quoted for giving me powerful words to add depth to this book and to a canon of "No One Size fits All" Motivational/Self-help writing.

To Visions, Inc., who taught me the foundational frameworks of my personal journey of liberation.

To my young adult offspring Gina and Teotli for making me dig deep every day so my actions match my words.

Virtual Appendix

There is so much I could refer you to and so much is added each day. I have a tab of resources on my website that I will keep updated. If you have others you wish me to add, please send me a message. My contact info and the Appendix tab is on my website: lindagonzalez.net